T0319031

Cambridge Elements ≡

Elements in Applied Evolutionary Science
edited by
David F. Bjorklund
Florida Atlantic University

EVOLUTIONARY PERSPECTIVES ON ENHANCING THE QUALITY OF LIFE

Mads Larsen
University of Oslo

Nina Witoszek
University of Oslo

THE EVOLUTION INSTITUTE

CAMBRIDGE
UNIVERSITY PRESS

CAMBRIDGE
UNIVERSITY PRESS

Shaftesbury Road, Cambridge CB2 8EA, United Kingdom

One Liberty Plaza, 20th Floor, New York, NY 10006, USA

477 Williamstown Road, Port Melbourne, VIC 3207, Australia

314–321, 3rd Floor, Plot 3, Splendor Forum, Jasola District Centre,
New Delhi – 110025, India

103 Penang Road, #05–06/07, Visioncrest Commercial, Singapore 238467

Cambridge University Press is part of Cambridge University Press & Assessment,
a department of the University of Cambridge.

We share the University's mission to contribute to society through the pursuit of
education, learning and research at the highest international levels of excellence.

www.cambridge.org
Information on this title: www.cambridge.org/9781009517270

DOI: 10.1017/9781009378543

When citing this work, please include a reference to the DOI 10.1017/9781009378543

First published 2024

A catalogue record for this publication is available from the British Library.

ISBN 978-1-009-51727-0 Hardback
ISBN 978-1-009-37853-6 Paperback
ISSN 2752-9428 (online)
ISSN 2752-941x (print)

Cambridge University Press & Assessment has no responsibility for the persistence
or accuracy of URLs for external or third-party internet websites referred to in this
publication and does not guarantee that any content on such websites is, or will
remain, accurate or appropriate.

Evolutionary Perspectives on Enhancing the Quality of Life

Elements in Applied Evolutionary Science

DOI: 10.1017/9781009378543
First published online: March 2024

Mads Larsen
University of Oslo

Nina Witoszek
University of Oslo

Author for correspondence: Mads Larsen, madla@uio.no

Abstract: Positive psychology is a thriving field with increasing political influence, yet there are few evolutionary studies that have had a tangible impact on rethinking mechanisms of well-being. This Element reviews existing literature and proposes synthesizing insights into human flourishing under an umbrella of multilevel selection (MLS). Conceptualizing quality of life as 'Happiness + Meaning = Well-being' draws attention to how people navigate between individual and group needs, and how they reconcile selfish pursuits with altruism and cooperation. We define happiness as the cluster of affects that reward individuals for solving adaptive challenges. We approach meaning as a reward that individuals experience when contributing to their community. By way of examples, we critically examine the Nordic well-being societies whose ethos and education advance prosocial values and practices and strike a balance between individualist and communitarian ideals. This title is also available as Open Access on Cambridge Core.

Keywords: evolutionary psychology, multilevel selection, positive psychology, prosociality, well-being

ISBNs: 9781009517270 (HB), 9781009378536 (PB), 9781009378543 (OC)
ISSNs: 2752-9428 (online), 2752-941x (print)

Contents

1 Introduction: The Battle of the Books in Well-Being Studies

How can we make happier lives for more people? In a growing number of developed countries, experts and politicians consider this a fundamental question. In the twenty-first century, people's subjective experience of their own quality of life has become a key metric for assessing policy. In 2011, the United Nations unanimously adopted the resolution 'Happiness: Toward a Holistic Approach to Development'. Secretary-General Ban Ki-moon declared that 'while material prosperity is important, it is far from being the only determinant of well-being'.[1] The *World Happiness Report* has since ranked nations based on the levels of citizens' overall sense of their perceived quality of life. Dozens of countries now deploy well-being accounts to supplement GDP and other economic measures (Diener et al., 2015; Durand, 2018).

The focus on 'gross national happiness' has been prompted by the growing realization that economic growth does not necessarily make people happier. Once national prosperity reaches a certain level – around $10,000 in GDP per capita – further growth has a limited effect on human flourishing (Kahneman et al., 1999). But policies focused on increasing general levels of well-being have suffered a few setbacks. The common modern assumption, that economic and technological progress would ensure 'the relief of man's estate' (Bacon, 1960 [1620]: xxvii), has been compromised in many post-industrial societies by such phenomena as growing social alienation and atomization,[2] increasing depression rates, and pharmacological excesses. There is now evidence to the effect that young people no longer embody the idea of joyful and carefree life; rather, they are becoming victims of debilitating anxiety and despair (Foa & Mounk, 2019; Hellevik & Hellevik, 2021).

If economic growth will only take us so far, what could we try instead? Well-being scholars strive to answer this question. Positive psychology has been a thriving field since a 1984 article by Ed Diener, the recently passed founder of subjective well-being studies (Bakshi, 2019). Research on well-being has been called the 'hottest topic in social science' (De Vos, 2012). But considering the scholarly and political focus on making people happier – and our growing knowledge on drivers of human flourishing – experts are surprisingly unable to prescribe and implement policies that work. Their powerlessness is predictable. In spite of neurobiological advances, human nature remains an enigma with regard to what really makes us flourish and prosper.

---

[1] On 2 April, 2012, in a meeting chaired by Jigmi Y. Thinley, the Prime Minister of Bhutan, and Jeffrey D. Sachs, the first *World Happiness Report* was presented to review evidence from the emerging science of happiness; see https://sustainabledevelopment.un.org/index.php?page=view&type=400&nr=617&menu=35.

[2] This atomization is more acute in authoritarian, than liberal, countries.

Most Western philosophers and psychologists refer to *happiness* as a value term, roughly synonymous with well-being or flourishing. In this reading, happiness is both an emotional and cognitive state involving positive experiences such as joy, love, curiosity, interest, and satisfaction. However, even a peremptory overview of the wealth of scholarly literature on well-being, shows a plethora of often contradictory definitions and conceptualizations. There are studies of *hedonic happiness* achieved through experiences of pleasure and enjoyment, and explorations of *eudaimonic happiness* gained through experiences of and purpose and harmony in one's life (Røysamb & Nes, 2016). Some psychologists talk about a *relational happiness*, dependent on positive (or negative) affects deriving from our interaction with family, friends, and strangers (e.g., Holmes & McKenzie, 2019; White, 2017).

Things are not made easier by philosophers, writers, and sages who have captured an often personalized, contextual nature of happiness. For Socrates, the key to happiness was self-knowledge. For Nietzsche, only cows were unequivocally happy; the great men could not be happy without suffering. Einstein supposedly believed that 'if you want to live a happy life, tie it to a goal, not to people or things'.[3] In short, happiness and well-being are 'mongrel concepts', to invoke Ned Block's (1995) apt formulation. Their uses and interpretations point to a mess. Similarly, the measuring of well-being is a subject of an ongoing controversy, though international ranking of countries of according to various – supposedly universal – happiness indicators have become an established practice of psychologists, UN commissions, and mushrooming happiness research institutions (Adler, 2019; Austin, 2015).

In this Element, we treat happiness as a positive, but often fleeting, affect which is but a component of a more comprehensive concept of well-being. We argue that well-being is a cumulative – cognitive and emotional – state involving happiness and a sense of direction or purpose – or meaning – which creates the durable basis of a fulfilled life. We can make do without enjoyment for a while, and even with little satisfaction. But if we lack the meaning of life – which often takes a lot of effort and sacrifice to find – we can be utterly lost. Without it, we cannot navigate life's inevitable challenges and crises. When we do have a sense of meaning, we can more easily face life with hope and inner peace, even in the most adverse conditions.

The notion of well-being is not only conceptually challenging. On a cultural level, it has become increasingly clear that the well-being field has relied too much on Western notions of what a good life should consist of. When the

---

[3] https://thomas-oppong.medium.com/why-einstein-said-if-you-want-to-live-a-happy-life-tie-it-to-a-goal-8063915f4515.

American Dream sanctified 'the pursuit of happiness', the project of maximizing pleasure and contentment became a transcultural aspiration. The United States Declaration of Independence portrayed such a pursuit as an unalienable right of all humans. But, as we know too well, there are always painful limits to unalienable rights, especially in the twenty-first-century United States.

Scepticism aside, for a long time it has been assumed that liberal democracy and individual rights were the keys to human flourishing. Diener contended that individualism is strongly predictive of well-being (Diener et al., 1995), a position with clear policy implications. Such West-centrism is now under siege. There is a growing strain of influential scholarly studies showing that Western perceptions of happiness have been too dominant and too intrusive in international indexes and rankings. There is now a more nuanced perception both of distinctive, cultural determinants of happiness, and of the ways in which positive psychologists have conceptualized and misconstrued well-being, be it in surveys or in qualitative research (Krys et al., 2021a, 2021b; Rappleye et al., 2020; Uchida & Kitayama, 2009; Uchida et al., 2009).

To mention but a few examples, in cultures influenced by Confucianism, well-being is more of an interpersonal concept. Since good relationships and social harmony are primary, it is assumed that well-being should be pursued in an interdependent manner, highlighting the role of roots and community as opposed to more independent and individualist Western avenues. In cultures where people are meant to do well together, individuals who pursue success and happiness on their own can be viewed as a threat to group flourishing. There is an increasing realization that in these cultural contexts, well-being should perhaps be assessed as a group phenomenon. Diener argued that the ways in which positive psychologists have measured well-being are 'inherently democratic' (Diener et al., 2009b), but, again, his concept of 'democratic' comes from a distinctly Western tradition (Henrich, 2020).

Individuals and cultures may also be averse to happiness. Some radical Buddhist schools of thought view a desire for happiness as misguided, if not outright harmful, much like the Western Puritans who closed theatres and abolished Christmas.[4] In the Muslim world, there are subcultures that associate happiness with sin and shallowness. Many East Asian societies regard happiness as often deriving from immoral motives and actions (Joshanloo & Weijers, 2014; Uchida et al., 2004). These perceptions present a stark contrast to the

---

[4] In 1647, the radically Puritan English Parliament outlawed Christmas services and the celebrations that went along with them; see www.historic-uk.com/HistoryUK/HistoryofEngland/Cromwell-Puritan-Christmas/; www.nyu.edu/about/news-publications/news/2022/december/who-waged-the-very-first–war-on-christmas–.html.

dominant Western views of individual happiness being closely entwined with satisfying individual appetites and aspirations (Braithwaite & Law, 1985).

World cultures represent a mosaic of multiple notions of the ideals of good life and human flourishing. Though space does not allow us to delve into detail, Hindu beliefs are especially intriguing as early intuitions and representations of evolution as a complex progress towards an ever-increasing well-being. The Hindu notion of the *Purusharthas* – or the fourfold path to human self-realization – seeks to create cultural conditions for the pursuit of the four goals of happy life: from the lower one, emphasizing sensuous and material pleasure (*kama*), through the pursuit of wealth and power (*artha*), ethical goodness (*dharma*), and on to attaining spiritual transcendence (*moksha*) (Parel, 2008: 41).

We shall return to the discussion of cultural determinants of well-being in successive sections. What well-being should entail, beyond covering basic needs, remains elusive. Scholars highlight a variety of possibly fundamental features, including the hedonistic (pleasure), eudaimonic (self-realization), cognitive (satisfaction), or objective (lists of goods) (Røysamb & Nes, 2016). Disagreement is also considerable with regard to well-being strategies. Should we really strive to maximize positive and minimize negative affect (Gruber et al., 2011)? Ideally, should everyone's ambition be to strive for everlasting happiness? Or was the Auschwitz survivor Victor Frankl right when he concluded, 'It is the very pursuit of happiness that thwarts happiness'?

Another conundrum is offered by the conflict between individual and social strategies as these relate to the quest for happiness. We must consider the fact that many important sources of happiness derive from competitive success, which can include schadenfreude at another's loss. If I successfully pursue happiness, I may outcompete you in a manner that makes you less happy. When I win my dream job, partner, or other rival goods, others do not. The saying 'comparison is the thief of joy' seems particularly accurate in this context. If happiness depends on doing relatively well, then almost all individuals who compare themselves with their neighbours or peers are doomed to feel as failures at some level. One cannot be better in all things.

Paradoxically, since in-group contests tend to have more losers than winners, encouraging people to try harder to win what makes them happy is likely to entail a reduction of society's overall happiness. More competition might drive economic growth, but this may not benefit society as a whole. According to the *Easterlin paradox* (Easterlin, 1974; Hellevik, 2011; Stevenson & Wolfers, 2008), an increase in GDP per capita is often not followed by an elevation of the population's overall sense of well-being. In our responses to income as a potential source of happiness, we resort to relative, rather than absolute, comparisons. An increase in national prosperity beyond $10,000 GDP/cap makes little difference for the population's well-being (Kahneman et al., 1999). By contrast, when individuals earn more money and members of their comparison group do not, the extra income can have a significant effect on the individual's subjective sense of well-being.

The relational aspects of affluence beg the question: if we derive happiness not from what we have, but from what we have that those in our comparison group don't have, are happiness pursuits a zero-sum game? If so, there would be little policymakers could do to increase a population's overall happiness. An evolutionary inquiry into this and other questions within positive psychology can shed new light on the complex dynamics between the human desire for well-being and a whole palette of factors, from genes and cultural perceptions, to the role of altruism and cooperation, as well as the quest for meaning.

1.1 Outline of Sections

In this Element, we investigate human well-being through the evolutionary lens and assess the potential of evolutionary insights to inform policy and institutions designed to maximize human flourishing. We critically review influential literature that highlights what some scholars consider to be both biological and cultural universals – such as collaboration and altruism – and their relation to well-being (Bowles & Gintis, 2013; Haidt, 2006; Sober & Wilson, 2013; Welzel, 2013; Wilson, 2015, 2019).

In Section 2, we explore a strain in research on happiness that highlights cultural differences with regard to the ideals of good life and developmental paths (Krys et al., 2021a, 2021b). Large efforts are underway to develop quantitative surveys that – unlike the *World Happiness Report* – privilege culturally sensitive approaches to human well-being, studying the uniqueness of diverse normative patterns and ideas of social development. The question of whether the culturally sensitive and universalist approaches are at loggerheads is perhaps spurious. We argue that these perspectives complement one another by shedding light both on the distinctive traditions within, and on meeting points between, cultures.

In Section 3, we discuss the relationship between well-being and the ideas of good life as they evolved over millennia and across cultures. In spite of the cultural variety of eudaemonic ideals, there are striking parallels between various traditions that associate the good life with balance, working for the good of others, and the importance of compassion. These similarities spring from cultural learning and cross-pollination, but they also have a source in the evolutionary sciences' idea of a shared human nature. The increasing evidence for the commonalities of human nature calls for revisiting the philosophical stance of cultural relativism, which undergirds the constructivist approaches of social anthropology and the humanities. We highlight the work of David Sloan Wilson's ProSocial agenda, as he comes closest to crafting a comprehensive vision of well-being as anchored in the ethos of work for the betterment of humanity and the planet.

In Section 3.2, we discuss an intriguing reversal in the dynamic relationship between the social and evolutionary sciences. Well into the twenty-first century, the agenda of the humanities and the social sciences rested on the idea of social improvement. Evolutionary biology was largely identified as the study of selfish genes that were taken to stand in the way of human moral advancement. In the last decades – while social scientists plunged into declinism –evolutionary thought moved to a hopeful history of humankind based on the salience of altruism, prosociality, and cooperation. What are the implications of this intellectual transition?

In Section 4, we present a novel, multilevel selection (MLS) model for well-being, which emphasizes how human evolution has occurred under two often conflicting pressures: individual and group selection. Individuals are incentivized to be selfish to outcompete in-group members. At the same time, individuals are compelled to cooperate with in-group members in order to strengthen the group for competition against other groups. We propose that it can be profitable to think of human well-being as having evolved to motivate individuals affectively to contribute both to their own and their group's success. Our contention in this Element is that approaching happiness and meaning as connected rather than disjointed involves a double-fold dividend. First, it counteracts a conceptual overabundance in the field of positive psychology. Second, it draws attention to how experiences of well-being help individuals manoeuvre between the potentially conflicting pressures of individual and group selection. We sum up these insights with the equation: 'Happiness + Meaning = Well-Being'.

Section 4 is supplemented with insights from seminal works of narrative psychology relevant for our focus on well-being and meaning. Jerome Bruner (1990) adds valuable narrative perspectives on the human search for meaning, as does Viktor Frankl (1946) with his groundbreaking work on logotherapy in the treatment of concentration camp survivors.

In Section 5, we draw attention to the Nordic countries – with Norway in the spotlight. We explore challenges to these nations' transition from being welfare states to becoming well-being societies. In the twenty-first century, Norway, Denmark, Sweden, Finland, and Iceland have increasingly let their policies be guided by a shifting emphasis from welfare, whose basis is largely socio-economic, to highlighting human well-being – that is, creating institutional structures for helping citizens to create better lives for themselves. An important part of Nordic policy has been to socialize citizens into engaging in altruistic activities. A shift from economic growth to concentrating on citizens' well-being is not without frictions but it is increasingly part of the Nordic governments' agenda.

In Section 6, we sum up our findings and reinspect the policy implications of applying the evolutionary lens to well-being. Both insights from the literature we scrutinized and our multilevel selection model of human well-being inform an integrative approach to human flourishing, one that draws attention to its non-zero-sum sources. Our purpose is to offer a cross-culturally applicable framework for well-being that can be used to identify which policies are most likely to create happier lives for more people.

2 A Century of Well-Being Studies

The earliest scientific happiness studies seem to have sprung from Abraham Myerson's efforts around WWI to establish a field of 'mental hygiene'. The Harvard neuropathologist referred to his programme of *eupathics* as 'the more gracious sister' of eugenics. Instead of eliminating the unfit, eupathics aimed for 'the well-being of the normal' (Myerson, 1917: 344). Myerson equated well-being with happiness, understood primarily as a positive mood. Systematic happiness research developed in the following decades. In the 1920s and 1930s, subjective measures were employed in marriage studies, educational psychology, and personality psychology. This methodology was further refined in research within mental health, gerontology, and the social indicator movement of the 1960s and 1970s (Angner, 2011).

After 1960, large surveys of happiness began sampling entire nations. A main concern was to identify which personal characteristics correlated with feeling good. Warner Wilson concluded that the happy individual is typically a 'young, healthy, well-educated, well-paid, extroverted, optimistic, worry-free, religious, married person with high self-esteem, high job morale, modest aspirations, of either sex, and of a wide range of intelligence' (Wilson, 1967: 294).[5] The complexity of survey results led researchers to conclude that happiness was not a uniform experience, but consisted of different affects driven by a variety of individual and social factors (Diener, 2009c).

The World Values Survey – administered in seven 'waves' from 1981 to 2020 – drove the emergence of global happiness studies. Over 100,000 respondents from around 100 nations have rated their life satisfaction on a 10-point scale. Since they also answered questions about values, income, education,

---

[5] It is worth noting that Wilson's study does not consider race.

relationship status, volunteer work, and political actions, well-being scholars have been able to identify a line of correlations across cultures (Oishi et al., 2009). Ed Diener's 1984 article in *Psychological Bulletin*, 'Subjective Well-Being', was a watershed moment for the field. In this highly cited paper, which was followed by a spurt in kindred publications (Khademi & Najafi, 2020), Diener outlined the state of the art for subjective well-being studies.

By the 2000s, well-being scholars felt that their field had achieved such a solid empirical grounding that their findings should inform political decisions. This was a significant change in aspirations. In 1984, Diener had insisted that well-being studies should be descriptive and that researchers should avoid normative claims. Similarly, Martin Seligman had concluded that 'science must be morally neutral' (Seligman, 2002: 129). But in 2004, Diener and Seligman argued, 'Our thesis is that well-being should become a primary focus of policymakers, and that its rigorous measurement is a primary policy imperative . . . Well-being ought to be the ultimate goal around which economic, health, and social policies are built' (Diener & Seligman, 2004: 1–2).

This change in ambitions coincided with a turn towards striving for greater objectivity in the assessment of well-being. Seligman advocated a more social understanding of human flourishing, as something that does not only exist inside the heads of individuals, but includes relationships and accomplishments. It is not enough that people feel that they are doing well; they should actually do well – compared to how other people are doing. Well-being was still understood primarily as a subjective experience, but increasingly became seen as also having an objective dimension (White, 2017). The pursuit of happiness should continue to be an individual endeavour, but governments would profit from getting more involved in facilitating access to those resources that made their citizens feel that they have better lives. This change in thinking set in motion the movement that culminated in the UN's 2011 resolution on happiness measures as the foundation for 'a holistic approach to development'.

2.1 Culturally Sensitive Approaches to Human Flourishing

There is a current within positive psychology which emphasizes the cultural relativity of well-being and insists on respecting cultural particulars. In WEIRD countries (Western, Educated, Industrialized, Rich, Democratic), it is taken for granted that individuals should pursue happiness. The proponents of the culturally sensitive approach argue that universalizing Western traits simplifies human diversity. Desiring a good life may be universal, but cultures understand happiness differently, emphasize distinct aspects of well-being, and have conflicting ideals as to what level of happiness is desirable. To what extent well-being is viewed as an individual or social phenomenon varies from culture to culture (Krys et al., 2021a, 2021b; Rappleye et al., 2020; Uchida & Kitayama, 2009; Uchida et al., 2009).

Positive psychologists representing the relativist position work on developing quantitative surveys that assess well-being across dozens of nations. Respondents' answers with regard to different aspects of well-being are weighted on the basis of their culture's specific preferences for what constitutes a good life. This allows for a ranking of nations more in line with cultural experiences, redolent of how purchasing power parity (PPP) functions for economic comparisons. An alternative World Happiness Report could see less of a Western dominance across its headline findings.

In our view, while cultural sensitivity is valuable in that it requires an eye for difference, it is also important to identify transcultural commonalities. Evolutionary perspectives can help uncover the predispositions that cultural differences build on, as well as make sense of seeming paradoxes. The fact that some cultures favour independent, individualistic happiness pursuits while others have a preference for interdependent, communal practices, is not a random result of history. What is adaptive varies with the cultural, political, and economic aspects of the environment.

Our modern environment consists of various levels of organization – from the interpersonal social group (e.g., family) to the impersonal moral group (e.g., nation) – often with overlapping constellations that we belong to on each level. We have family groups, kin groups, social groups, professional groups, interest groups, voluntary groups, geographically and politically delineated groups, and many others. These groups can have shared and conflicting interests. The level of individual independence within these collectives varies from culture to culture.

At the conceptual level, we can still draw a clear distinction between pressures of individual and group selection, even in those environments in which individuals are more dependent on their social collective to succeed. In kinship societies, the well-being of the kin group is of such importance to each member's fitness that interdependent, collectivistic concerns take precedence (Henrich, 2020). In most Western cultures, individual strategies are paramount. A culturally sensitive approach to well-being could still define happiness as related to individual selection yet recognize that distinct cultural values incentivize diverse strategies in terms of social organization when individuals solve adaptively relevant challenges. We suggest how to investigate these dynamics in Section 6.2.

In environments that make social groups especially important for individual flourishing, our evolutionary perspective predicts that members of a group benefit when each individual's well-being system is synchronized with those of the other members. This perspective illuminates why interdependent happiness assessments focus on how individuals feel in relation to other group members (Hitokoto & Uchida, 2015). To respond to signals of opportunity or threat, groups form collectivist cultures so that they can feel well or ill together – at least to a greater extent than in individualistic cultures. Happiness still relates to individual selection, but must be shared among more people – one's in-group – to optimize for adaptivity. The quantitative challenge is to operationalize such insights in cross-cultural surveys.

3 Ideas of Good Life: Are There Cultural Universals?

Jonathan Haidt draws on ancient and modern sources that help us understand what is required for humans to flourish. In *The Happiness Hypothesis: Finding Modern Truth in Ancient Wisdom* (2006), he concludes that one of positive psychology's most important ideas is the happiness formula of Lyubomirsky et al. (2005): $H = S + C + V$. H stands for happiness, S denotes your biological set point, C is about the conditions of your life, and V represents voluntary activities. The field's challenge is to find which conditions, in combination with which activities, are most likely to increase happiness for individuals in light of their biological and cultural heritage.

Haidt draws attention to happiness as a common topic of cosmologies, founding myths, and folklore all over the world. He echoes Amartya Sen (1993, 2016), arguing that people's ideas of what constitutes a good life reveal more similarities than differences. Three roads to happiness have been especially influential: (1) getting what you want, (2) a sense of well-being coming from within, and (3) well-being drawn from relations between people and working for the welfare of others. Sen and Haidt agree that the ideal of an egoistic pursuit of materially anchored happiness, however influential, has, in history, been eclipsed by more compelling parables of compassion and goodness in most cultures.

An emphasis on empathy and compassion as the basis of a good life was part of the ancient wisdom of *The Bhagavad Gita*, Confucius' *Analects*, The *Tao Te Ching*, Buddhist teachings, Greek and Roman philosophers such as Epictetus and Seneca, and the *New Testament*. Despite differences in details, these diverse conceptions of the good and meaningful life share an ethical platform which comprises such values as balance, the search for harmony, and selfless work for others.

In *The Bhagavad Gita*, from the second millennium BCE, Krishna counsels Arjuna to be compassionate to friend and enemy alike, to see himself in every person, and to suffer the sorrow of others as his own (6:32). Interestingly, the *Gita* does not ask for the enjoyment of life to be renounced; it advises against clinging to a selfish pursuit of happiness regardless of the cost to others. Selfless action leads to *self-realization*, which should not be confused with compensation for good deeds. Rather, altruistic practices help us liberate compassion, which is intrinsic to being human (53–4). Living the good life is about overcoming lower energies such as *tamas* (inertia) and *rajas* (self-centred action) and evolving towards selflessness and empathy. Implicit in this worldview is the belief that two forces pervade human existence: the downward pull of our past and the upward thrust of evolution (61).

According to Hindu religion, all living beings – humans, animals, and plants – evolve in their own ways towards light and delight. However, by choosing wrong actions, humans may devolve and descend into the lower worlds, being reborn as plants or animals and, in extreme cases, degenerate into demons and evil spirits. That said, nothing is predetermined: the lower beings can be reborn and given a chance of ascending to higher life forms through good actions, compassion, and forgiveness. The ultimate human purpose is reaching *moksha* – a sense of complete peace and balance, variously described as self-actualization, self-transcendence, self-liberation, complete enlightenment, or supreme consciousness (Agarval, 2000; Klostermeier, 2004; Kuppuswamy, 1977; Mendis, 1994).

Representations of the good life as work for the common good that leads to self-actualization can be detected in the ideas of Ashoka the Great, the Mauryan ruler in the region of present-day India and Pakistan, who lived in the third century BCE. In his Dhamma edict, Ashoka described his mobilization of magistrates and officials to work for the 'welfare, happiness, and benefit of the people':

> Wherever medical herbs suitable for humans or animals are not available, I have had them imported and grown. Along roads I have had wells dug and trees planted for the benefit of humans and animals ... Truly, I consider the welfare of all to be my duty, and the root of this is exertion and the prompt dispatch of business. There is no better work than promoting the welfare of all the people and whatever efforts I am making is to repay the debt I owe to all beings to assure their happiness in this life, and attain heaven in the next.[6]

We refer to these ancient sources for two reasons. First, they point to the often-underestimated process of cultural learning and cross-pollination in social development and individual improvement. Many of the ideas of the *Gita*, such as self-realization and compassionate selfless identification with all living

---

[6] http://faculty.wartburg.edu/lindgrene/edicts_of_king_ashoka%20revised.htm.

beings, found their way into the twentieth-century Deep Ecology as advocated by the Norwegian ecosopher Arne Næss. Second, as we shall see, some of the *Gita*'s motifs resonate with evolutionary research, especially David Sloan Wilson's ProSocial vision.

A prosocial strain of current evolutionary thought highlights how pressures of group selection have driven the creation of culture that compels individuals to collaborate and sacrifice for others. The evolutionary interest in well-being is interesting for positive psychology for several reasons. (1) A perspective of gene/culture interplay in human development acknowledges the power of cultural values – and therefore also politics and economics – in shaping human well-being. (2) Coevolution draws attention to the fertile relationship between selfishness and prosociality, and competition and cooperation, as preconditions of well-functioning democracies with high quality of life. (3) While not dismissing cultural differences, such prosocial evolutionary thinking stresses the shared biological and cultural inheritance of all humans, thus challenging the tenets of radical relativism in cultural studies.

The salience of empathy, compassion, and acceptance in this accumulated transcultural wisdom is striking. It testifies to the fact that ideas of happiness and well-being are not carved in stone in any culture. They are subject to constant negotiation and – more often than not – stem from diverse cultural borrowings and inspirations.

3.1 Enter Evolutionary Science

In the 2000s, David Buss, a pioneer of evolutionary psychology, and Randolph Nesse, a pioneer of evolutionary medicine, made valuable contributions to positive psychology. Buss (2000) concluded that modernity detracts from people's happiness primarily due to environmental mismatch and larger comparison groups. We live in a more prosperous environment, but this fact does not undermine that there can be a benefit to feeling distress when our adaptive strategies fail, as such emotions signal that we should change our strategies.

Nesse (2005) elaborated on the adaptive functions of positive and negative emotions, which explains why these affects evolved. He proposed that an evolutionary approach could offer a theoretical bridge from which we can better understand human emotions as they relate to goal pursuit, as well as suggest policies that align with our desires and predispositions. Hill and Buss (2008) noted that with the field's high stakes, it was 'surprising that few researchers have yet to explore subjective well-being from an evolutionary perspective'. Only sporadic contributions have since been made. Evolutionary scholars have researched the drivers of human flourishing and discontent – for instance

Gluckman and Hanson's *Mismatch* (2006) – but rarely within the field of positive psychology. A notable exception is *Positive Evolutionary Psychology* (Geher & Wedberg, 2019), which offers an overview of psychological predispositions and their relevance to human thriving. In *Introduction to Positive Evolutionary Psychology* – which is part of the same Element series as our Element – Geher et al. (2023) illustrate the utility of applying evolutionary thinking to positive psychology.

Many evolutionary scholars' focus on the largely negative sources of human well-being – such as selfishness and self-interest – is something of a puzzle. By way of speculation, the hegemony of the selfish gene theory could be explained, at least in part, through the strength of logos, ethos, and pathos in the narratives emphasizing selfishness. The logos had to do with Richard Dawkins' (1976) masterly, scientifically grounded narrative, anchored in the dominant behaviourist theories and pointing to selfishness as the ultimate motif all human pursuits, including acts of altruism. But the pathos and ethos played a possible role as well; in the era when Dawkins' book was published, the promotion of individual, egoistic ends coincided with the rise of neoliberal ideals marshalled by influential thinkers such as Friedrich Hayek, Milton Friedman, and Ayn Rand. There were, of course, alternative views: the great philosopher Mary Midgley (2010), we recall, criticized the selfish gene theory for presenting a one-sided, reductionist view of humans as ruled by self-interest alone, and for threatening to legitimate, even fetishize, neoliberal individualism as the basis of human well-being.

When seen in this context, evolutionary science's interest in cooperation and prosociality has marked a seeming paradigm shift. We write 'seeming' because the shift has been less a dramatic breakthrough and more a scholarly *ricorso*: a return to strains and ideas that had been subjects of earlier scholarly studies. Illuminating examples are Lee Dugatkin's *Cooperation Among Animals: An Evolutionary Perspective* (1977) and Robert Axelrod's *The Evolution of Cooperation* (1984). More importantly, many ideas that emerge from modern labs working on animal cooperation gesture towards evolutionary theories by Peter Kropotkin. When Kropotkin undertook an epic journey through Siberia in the 1860s, the evolutionary orthodoxy advanced that the natural world was a brutal place. And yet, instead of nature red in tooth and claw, Kropotkin found countless examples of mutual aid within species, as well as evidence of the superiority of groups that practiced altruism and cooperation. A close observation of the behaviour of migrating birds, mammals, fish schools, and insect societies made him conclude that a driving evolutionary force behind all social life – be it in microbes, animals, or humans – was the law of mutual aid (Woodcock & Avakumović, 1950).

From our present-day perspective, Kropotkin's findings were of course incomplete – and as one-sided as Dawkins' theory of selfish genes. But they paved the way for a careful rereading of Darwin's ideas and rebalancing the studies of evolutionary biology, anthropology, and psychology through complementing the focus on ruthless competition with studies of empathy and altruism as sources of human well-being.

Buss and Nesse limited themselves to studying well-being mostly from a perspective that connects happiness to in-group competition – that is, individual selection. When we solve adaptively relevant challenges – those that ultimately promote our survival and reproduction – we are rewarded by positive feelings that motivate us to repeat such behaviour. Unhappiness evolved to tell us that our strategies are failing and that we need to change course. Feelings of happiness can be viewed as a compass that steers us towards successes that exceed those of our comparison group. Yet this is only one part of the equation. Considerable well-being can be derived from altruistic behaviour that does not directly enhance fitness for the altruist (Dolan et al., 2008; Meier & Stutzer, 2008; Musick & Wilson, 2003; Piliavin, 2003; Thoits & Hewitt, 2001).

Roy Baumeister's work on meaning illuminates how positive affects evolved to reward people for contributing to their community (Baumeister, 2005; Baumeister et al., 2013). Acting in line with cultural ideals – such as helping others – offers the altruist a sense of meaning that can have a more lasting effect on their well-being than the happiness rush that is typically derived from winning in-group competitions. The term *hedonistic treadmill* refers to how successful happiness pursuits often only lead to a temporary increase in well-being (Diener et al., 2009b). This is another apparent paradox of positive psychology, which an evolutionary perspective can help illuminate.

The pursuit of meaning can – in contrast to happiness quests – engender a sense of self-esteem and social belonging. It can also transform individual identity, elevating the altruist's quality of life for months or years. Success in such pursuits also tends to be more available, as helping others is a less competitive field. Our drive for meaning, which is uniquely human, offers a win-win source of well-being, one that benefits the altruists, those they help, and the community they all belong to. Cultures able to compel individuals to aid in-group members gain advantages in terms of group selection.[7] A community in which people take care of each other will have more resourceful members and greater cohesion than one dominated by selfishness (Wilson & Hessen, 2018).

---

[7] Steven Pinker (2015) argues that *group selection* likely has not had a genetic effect, but that the term functions as a metaphor for cultural advantages.

3.2 Evolutionary Thinkers as World Improvers

The idea that anything altruistic is cultural and anything selfish is biological would be a gross simplification. Empathy is not just a cultural construct; it is certainly useful at the biological level in the sense that those who are driven to care for their family and friends assist with the survival of those family and friends and thus increase their own fitness and survival when that altruism is reciprocated. Similarly, an excessive focus on the self, together with the promotion of selfish behaviour, does not exclusively spring from selfish genes. In a country like the United States, selfishness has become a cultural hallmark, an ostensible condition of a successful and happy life.

In this context, the agenda of social improvement highlighted by the prosocial wave of evolutionary thought marks an intriguing turn.[8] Evolutionary theory as preached and practiced by such thinkers as Frans De Waal or David S. Wilson is no longer associated with legitimizing the 'demonic' side of modernity. Exit imperialism, racism, and colonial might-is-right. Enter the survival of the friendliest and kindest. The synergy between biology and historical-cultural perspectives has produced a new narrative: evolution is not just a parade of selfish genes, but also progress towards altruism and prosociality. This is an interesting trend because it runs counter to a deluge of social science studies focused on the multiple, and seemingly irresolvable, crises of our time such as the apparent death of democracy, and even a descent to a New Middle Ages (Wooldridge, 2020). In defiance of these apocalyptic scenarios, Rutger Bregman argues in *Humanity: A Hopeful History*, 'It's when crisis hits when the bombs fall or the floodwaters rise – that we humans become our best selves' (2019: 4).

Bregman contributes to a growing body of literature which offers a positively charged, optimistic view of human potential. The idea that humans are hardwired primarily for selfishness and ruthless competition has been challenged by Frans de Waal (2010). He argues that the success of *Homo sapiens* rests to a significant extent on our capacity for empathy and our urge to understand and appreciate others. While being competitive, humans also possess an innate sensitivity to the emotional status of other members of our species. De Waal cites the consensus among biologists that empathy arrived with the evolution of maternal care in mammals. Crucial to this process was the controlling role of the hormone oxytocin, which induces empathy in males and females alike.[9]

---

[8] https://thisviewoflife.com/three-waves-of-evolutionary-thought/.
[9] In studies of cooperative and competitive behaviour among a group of men and women, both groups were sprayed with oxytocin, which led to an increase in trust and empathy; see McKie (2010).

Chimpanzees care for mates who are wounded by leopards. Elephants offer 'reassuring rumbles' to youngsters in distress. Dolphins guide sick companions to near the water's surface to prevent them from drowning.

The well-being of many animals and humans is the result of an emotional contagion: a happy and joyful environment is likely to generate happy and joyful individuals. Empathy holds our societies together, drives us to look after the sick, and makes us more flexible under stress. Through a better understanding of empathy's survival value in evolution, de Waal suggests, we advance a less simplistic and more accurate view of the complexity of human nature that allows us to work together towards a more just and flourishing society.

A similarly upbeat view of human development is championed by evolutionary psychologist Steven Pinker (2012, 2019). Probing into the adaptive functions of our cognitive and emotional systems, Pinker documents how parts of humanity have progressed from violent tribalism to modern human-rights societies. He uses a telescopic, historical perspective to argue that the images of violence and misery peddled by contemporary media do not give an accurate picture of human development. Using empirical evidence and ample statistics, he substantiates how the present era is less violent, less cruel, and more conducive to nurturing human well-being than any previous period. Most people today are not only less likely to meet a violent death; they are increasingly able to seek happiness and self-realization.[10]

Pinker reveres the Enlightenment, which he defines as the triumph of humanism and scientific breakthroughs. It was in the time of the *Lumières* that people gradually began to question forms of violence that had previously been taken for granted: slavery, torture, despotism, duelling, and extreme forms of cruel punishment. The ensuing decrease in suffering contributed to greater well-being. Countless individuals from across the world escaped honour killings, retaliations, and the traumas of religious persecution, setting out to search for happiness. The American dream was born.

Needless to say, Pinker's one-eyed, Cyclopean vision of the Enlightenment has been the subject of many critical assaults for its inaccurate account of inequality and a cavalier attitude to the dark sides of modern globalization (Goldin, 2018). The eighteenth century's progress was not just about reason and science. It was inseparably connected to Western empire-building, and the selected horrors of the Industrial Revolution, whose advocates preached and practiced slavery, genocide, exploitation, and racism. Ironically, this murky Enlightenment – or Endarkenment – sought legitimation for its inhumanity by

---

[10] Supporting his contention with abundant comparative statistics, Pinker argues that one's chance of being murdered is now less than one-tenth, and in some countries only one-fiftieth, of what it would have been if one had lived 500 years ago.

quoting evolutionary science, in its Spencerian version, and the laws of nature.[11]

Despite this massive criticism, Pinker's stance on the advancement towards a kinder world has remained heroically unflinching. It is hard to disagree, he argues, that – in a relatively short time – many societies have come far from the days when lynchings were commonplace, torture was ubiquitous, women were treated as cattle, and children were put to hard work at the age of seven. What about the civilizational collapse caused by the unspeakable horrors of Nazi and Bolshevik death factories? Even here, Pinker insists, violence was 'no more extreme' than the massive genocide and mayhem caused, say, by thirteenth-century Mongol conquests that led to the deaths of an estimated forty million people – not far from the more than fifty-five million who died in World War II; and this was in a world with only one-seventh of the population of the mid-twentieth century.

Pinker's lofty argument is that after World War II, most Western countries experienced the 'long peace', marked by the 'rights revolution', and growing revulsion against violence inflicted on ethnic minorities, women, children, sexual minorities, and even nature. Despite the ongoing conflicts, the ideal of eudaimonic happiness has taken hold of the imagination of people from all over the world; witness the narrative about the 'slumdog millionaire' in an award-winning Indian blockbuster. Its message of hope and redemption sent to the wretched inhabitants of Indian slums invokes a classic American narrative of the rise from rags to riches. But the film is not, as some critics contend, a re-branding of the American dream as Indian and sending it back to the West. Rather, in our view, it is about the universal human longing for happiness, prosperity, freedom, and recognition – a quest whose modern version was codified in a multiethnic society like the United States.

Genetic evolution can hardly explain these rapid changes, reasons Pinker. Evolution shaped the basic design of our brain, but it also equipped us with our cognitive and emotional faculties, which have been invested into cultural norms and values. The result is that propensities for violence – our 'inner demons' – exist side by side with 'the better angels of our nature' (Abraham Lincoln's words) that incline us to be peaceful and cooperative. It is our material circumstances and existential constraints, along with the working of morally charged cultural values and practices, that determine whether the demons or the angels gain the upper hand.

---

[11]   As late as the early twentieth century, John D. Rockefeller referred to the predatory expansion of big businesses as 'merely the working out of a law of nature', exemplifying a view of human nature that was as erroneous as it was toxic in fuelling self-fulfilling prophecies; see Austin (1988: 993).

3.3 Cooperative and Reciprocal Humans on a Path to Eudaimonia

A preoccupation with the pivotal importance of altruism and cooperation in human evolution is increasingly penetrating interdisciplinary scholarship. Evolution may have created 'selfish genes', as Richard Dawkins (1976) would have it, but this is only one part of a more complex picture. Citing Adam Smith's *Theory of Moral Sentiments*, Darwin (1874) argued that the

> basis of sympathy lies in our strong retentiveness of former states of pain or pleasure. [Hence] the sight of another person enduring hunger, cold, fatigue, revives in us some recollection of these states, which are painful even in idea. We are thus impelled to relieve the sufferings of another, in order that our own painful feelings may be at the same time relieved. In like manner we are led to participate in the pleasures of others.

Brian Hare and Vanessa Woods (2020), who examined the meaning of Spencer's 'survival of the fittest', argue that this term cannot be reduced to 'dog eats dog'. Darwin's theory of evolution is as much about individual competition as it is about cooperation, symbiosis, and reciprocity. Friendliness and cooperation rather than dominance, Hare and Woods insist are the keys to evolutionary survival. Modern evolutionary biologists have entered into a fruitful cooperation with economists, anthropologists, archaeologists, and psychologists who provide empirical evidence for social cooperation as one of the core conditions for the survival of the species (Buchanan & Powell, 2018; Corning, 2012; Haidt, 2006; Henrich, 2017; Richerson & Boyd, 2005; Sober & Wilson, 2013; Welzel, 2013).

Insights from evolutionary psychology (Cosmides & Tooby, 2013), cross-cultural psychology (Ryan & Deci, 2017), evolutionary anthropology (Richerson & Boyd, 2005), clinical psychology (Hayes et al., 2020), and experimental philosophy (Guglielmo et al., 2009) indicate that certain human proclivities, such as a thirst for freedom and fairness, derive from evolutionary root principles that relate to all cultures. Christian Welzel (2013) contends that an emancipative drive is universal, constituting the motivational source of human empowerment, which – in the last instance – increases people's well-being.

This emancipative trajectory does not imply a linear process. Our urge for freedom is countered by a desire for security. Our quest for justice is offset by the human penchant for ruthless domination. Our ability to cooperate is countered by our compulsion to compete. The works we reviewed in the previous paragraphs argue that these opposing drives are evolutionary universals. The prominence of one or the other trait in dominant cultural narratives has a bearing on societies' predicament and the well-being of their members. Cultures that advocate tolerance and social inclusion have high levels of human flourishing.

Those that promote a competitive-sectarian ethos often succumb to social polarization that can make nations, tribes, and empires crumble (Turchin, 2007).

Cultural evolution is a zig-zag process replete with advancements and regressions. Sophisticated Etruscan and Harappan civilizations were vanquished by muscular barbarians. The tolerant European Enlightenment was for decades eclipsed by Fascism and Bolshevism. Yet in each case, cooperative and pro-social societies resurfaced and rebuilt themselves after multiple traumas. There are several explanations for these resurrections. One is the evolutionary pull of prosocial moral sentiments, meaning that groups predisposed to cooperate and uphold ethical norms tend to survive and expand relative to more selfish groups.

Numerous studies contend that despite setbacks, the advancement towards modern, happier societies has been dependent on cultural values that foreground cooperation, altruism, fairness, and emancipative aspirations (Corning, 2011; Haidt, 2006; Ricard, 2015; Welzel, 2013; Wilson, 2016; Wilson & Hessen, 2015). Research on 170 societies shows that feelings of freedom enhance a population's life satisfaction. In *Freedom Rising*, Welzel (2013) portrays happiness as being founded on a 'ladder of freedoms', which is highly dependent on people's level of existential stress. If evolution has instilled in humans an adaptive quest for liberty, this drive can hibernate under authoritarian pressures but awaken when existential opportunities widen.

Welzel makes a strong case for the connection between emancipative aspirations and well-being. The human search for freedom is universal, he insists, and this drive becomes stronger the more prosperous a population becomes. The theoretical foundation of his approach –and its evolutionary roots – is described as 'the utility ladder of freedoms'. To support his claims, Welzel quotes data from World Values Survey that show that societies with the highest levels of social emancipation are also the top scorers on global well-being indexes.

Rich, first-hand accounts mapping human behaviour in extreme situations concur that cooperative, rather than selfish, practices were crucial in the struggle for survival (Frankl, 1946; Levi, 1996; Pawełczyńska, 1979). These accounts lend support to David Sloan Wilson's argument (2016) to the effect that people cooperate not only for self-interest, but because they are genuinely concerned about the well-being of others. Many value behaving ethically for its own sake. Contributing to the success of a joint project, which benefits one's group, even at a personal cost, is tied to stronger feelings of self-respect and personal integrity. Altruism can evoke a sense of pride and even elation, as the account of our qualitative study in Section 4.4 shows.

In *Altruism: The Power of Compassion to Change Yourself and the World*, Matthieu Ricard (2015) traces the evolution of altruism across six million years. He argues against Dawkins who insisted that 'universal love and the welfare of the species as a whole are concepts that simply do not make evolutionary sense. [We must therefore] teach our children altruism, for we cannot expect it to be part of their biological nature' (1976: 2, 150). According to Ricard, Dawkins overlooks that humans are so driven to help others that they often do so even when altruistic activities generate distressing emotions.

Samuel Bowles and Herbert Gintis (2013) pursue a similar line of reasoning in *A Cooperative Species: Human Reciprocity and Its Evolution*. Since cooperation was so crucial for survival, humans evolved the capacity for suppressing short-sighted selfish interest through developing ethical norms. Communities created institutions to protect the generous from being exploited by the selfish. The evolution of feelings such as guilt and shame underpinned our capacity for turning social norms into personal ideals. Groups with culture effective at promoting such processes would typically win in contests against groups marked by greater selfishness.

There are other strains of coevolution-inspired studies that link human well-being to our innate desire for fairness and freedom. In *The Fair Society* (2011) and *Superorganism* (2023), Peter Corning argues that we need what he calls 'a new bio-social contract' that assures human survival in the age of socio-environmental crises. In order to flourish, humanity needs to reduce inequality via redistribution of resources and creating fair forms of social organization which rest on the principles of equality, equity, and reciprocity.

There is one more determinant of well-being – elaborated in Section 4 – which has been illuminated in the work of the Harvard psychologist Jerome Bruner (1990, 1996). Bruner's cultural psychology challenged the behaviourist paradigm and biological determinism dominant in cognitive psychology of the 1950s and early 1960s. More importantly in the context of our study, it points to a close relationship between human self-realization, cultural narratives, and the search for meaning.[12] Culture is 'the way of life and through that we construct, negotiate, institutionalize, and finally (after it's all settled) end up calling "reality" to comfort ourselves' (Bruner, 1996: 87). Narratives that we spin to order and interpret the confusing world out there do not emerge in a vacuum. Tales are powerful psychological tools that come from our cultures and create paths to our well-being or to desolation and distress. Our well-being is thus a function of culturally entrenched stories we tell about ourselves and about others. According to Bruner, our immediate experience – and the meaning of our life – is framed in a narrative way. Negatively charged or constraining stories that we repeat to ourselves can make us feel lost and helpless. Our

---

[12] https://ioelondonblog.wordpress.com/2016/07/13/jerome-bruner-a-life-is-a-work-of-art-prob ably-the-greatest-one-we-produce/.

unhappiness may thus stem from a narrative 'neurosis' – a reflection of an insufficient, incomplete, or inappropriate story about ourselves. Empowering stories turn us into agents of our fate, guide us on a path to meaning and direction of our lives that, in turn, make us prosper and flourish.

The interaction between of a meaning-saturated culture and individual well-being is a complex process. On the one hand, the meaning we derive from our shared stories ties our groups together (Larsen, 2020). Thus, the narratives that guide us need to be shared to offer adaptive advantage. On the other hand, meaning is as much a part of the collective commons as it is shaped by unique individuals. The two do not always chime. When what we do or experience deviates from dominant cultural norms or stories, our well-being may suffer. Individuals who derive meaning from narratives and practices that cannot be synchronized with the worldview of their community, risk becoming branded as outcasts or heretics (it is enough to think of such famous cases as Socrates, Giordano Bruno, or Spinoza). That said, cultural norms and values are hardly ever switched off. On the contrary, even those individuals who defy traditions testify to the potency of entrenched habits of the heart and mind. The narrative construction of human well-being as intricately tied to meaning presents an ongoing and understudied challenge to positive psychology.

To sum up: Human biology makes up the foundation for how we experience well-being, but affects that are triggered by our prosocial behaviour are mediated through culture. Most individuals, who live up to the ideals of the cultural scripts into which we have been culturized, feel that their lives have meaning. The question is: What if stories cherished by the community makes it passive or reinforce disempowerment, since happiness and well-being are determined by God, emperor, or vengeful spirits? How to reconcile mobilizing stories that impel people to actively improve their lives with the entrenched, value-charged narratives that offer security in a chaotic world, even at the cost of individual happiness or freedom?

At the beginning of the new millennium, there has been a wealth of studies attempting to answer this question. In *Born to Be Good: The Science of a Meaningful Life* (Keltner, 2009), kindness to others and to oneself is the key to a happy life. In *Spiritual Evolution: How We Are Wired for Faith, Hope, and Love* (Vaillant, 2009), the cultivation of hope and love ensures that humans will evolve into more caring and spiritual beings. This is not just empty rhetoric.[13] In *Together: The Rituals, Pleasures, and Politics of Cooperation*, Richard Sennett (2013) urges that we reclaim and redesign our cooperative skills. Today, we share

---

[13] There are modern educational institutions, such as the International Baccalaureate School in Oslo, that use 'transformative learning' to promote care teamwork and hope as tools for overcoming the 'paralysis of enormity' tied to a cascade of modern crises.

space and institutions with people of different cultures, ethnicities, classes, and religions. Such diversity requires novel approaches to the challenges of prosociality. To minimize the risk of tribalism undermining everyone's well-being, we must learn to listen and debate rather than fight and squabble. Perfecting the art of cooperation to meet the challenges of our time, Sennett argues, is a crucial condition not only for human well-being but also for saving the planet.

The human search for happiness is like a river that never dries out. Even in situations that Hannah Arendt (1951) defined as the fruit of 'radical evil', dreams of well-being, however unattainable, do not die. Similarly, Viktor Frankl (1946), an Auschwitz survivor, and the author of *Man's Search for Meaning*, argued that self-transcendence in the act of helping others was often crucial for survival. In the most gruesome of circumstances, Frankl witnessed how people derived a minuscule amount of well-being from religion or brave altruistic acts that kept them going and endowed their life-in-death with meaning. As Nietzsche wrote, 'He who has a *why* to live can bear almost any *how*.'

In 2022, we interviewed a North Korean dissident who told us that, as a child, he had been brainwashed into believing that Kim Il Sung was God and that 'it was completely wrong and punishable to help one another'. After his parents had eloped to China, abandoning him to a life on the street, our North Korean informant still experienced occasional acts of kindness and compassion, such as a piece of bread being thrown to him by a fellow brother under the cover of night.

Psychologists who study patients with profound traumas argue that meaning cannot be generated from talking or argumentative thinking, only from actions and strong beliefs. In times of unspeakable horror, humans search for a modicum of well-being in selfless acts, turning to religion, or confirming one's humanity via mental or spiritual exercises (Hillman, 1994). After the war, Frankl used his experiences in the extermination camps to create a meaning-making *logotherapy*, a method for helping severely traumatized patients reclaim the purpose of their lives and which could be used to imagine and build a livable, post-apocalyptic future.

3.4 David Sloan Wilson's Prosociality: A Key to Planetary Well-Being

One of the most interesting, if controversial, contributions of evolutionary science to the study of human well-being has been made by David Sloan Wilson's 'ProSocial World' programme, a bold, research-based and practice-oriented agenda that promotes 'productive, equitable, and collaborative groups'.[14] The ProSocial programme is based on countless publications, conversations with

---

[14] www.prosocial.world/people/david-sloan-wilson.

world sages such as His Holiness the Dalai Lama, and concrete educational projects at local schools, playgrounds, and parks. The programme is as adventurous as it is breathtaking. Although Wilson prefers to talk about prosociality rather than well-being, it is clear that he treats the collaborative and altruistic ethos as a proxy of – and the path to – human flourishing. Genetics may have revolutionized our understanding of evolution in the twentieth century, but in our crisis-ridden times, Wilson contends, we need to push evolution beyond its genetic basis. We must reinforce evolutionary insights with historical and cultural research to find new ways of social improvement at both the local and global levels.

Relying on a perspective of multilevel selection, Wilson acknowledges that evolution on the individual level favours self-preservatory selfishness. At the same time, he shows that in the broader context, investing only in competitive winners can be counterproductive. Prioritizing exceptional individuals could undermine productivity and well-being in a variety of spheres, from animal breeding to the functioning of complex societies. Both in animal and human environments, having too many rapacious and self-centred individuals tears apart the social fabric upon which everyone relies.

Predictably, Wilson rejects *Homo economicus* as hardly conducive to fostering human flourishing. While not denying that happiness may spring from the fulfilment of one's selfish desires, Wilson's ProSocial framework is based on a narrative about human well-being as anchored in altruist and collaborative work, as well as in innovation and creativity. More importantly, in terms of policy implications, evolution is not top-down design but bottom-up adaptation and experimentation, as is the norm in biological systems. In Wilson's amplified biocultural perspective, important drivers of social change and advancement are small businesses, civic associations, localities, and nonprofits. In contrast to big, overly bureaucratized structures, small groups incentivize groundbreaking innovation and promote what works.

Wilson's biocultural perspective has been the subject of a lively controversy. It has been assaulted as being utopian, based on incomplete evidence, and involving methodological hazards in transmuting evolutionary biology into social science. Yet historical evidence – especially that furnished with Peter Turchin's data collected by the Seshat programme[15] – shows how the drive towards selfishness and sectarian tribalism in history has often resulted in a war of all against all, produced traumas, and, ultimately, social collapse. Similarly, *Homo economicus* may win against other members of their own tribe, but the

---

[15] https://peterturchin.com/publications/seshat-the-global-history-databank/; see also www.project-seshat.org.

selfish tribe mostly loses to cooperative groups which are more open to creativity and altruism.

In *This View of Life: Completing the Darwinian Evolution*, Wilson (2019) presents a progressive vision of human complexity increasing over the aeons, as bands become clans, clans become tribes, and tribes become nations. Inspired by the now largely forgotten ideas of Pierre Teilhard de Chardin, the twentieth-century evolutionary biologist, Jesuit priest, and philosopher, Wilson contends that evolution includes expansion of human consciousness towards an 'Omega Point'. The omega point of human consciousness gestures towards a moral community of people working for the good of the planet. That is the ultimate goal of the ProSocial programme: to create and refine a compelling, science-based vision – complete with cultural and educational tools and political strategies – to make humans better stewards of their own well-being and the well-being of Mother Earth. In short, *This View of Life* frames the evolutionary worldview as an ethical, even Promethean, project.

This Prometheanism is not without risk. Viewing evolutionary sciences as a key to what Wilson calls 'managing the future' through mastery of evolutionary processes (Wilson et al., 2014: 416) carries a danger of making evolutionary science into a tool of social engineering. Digital modernity – with its focus on AI, the biological hacking of humans, and a line of other innovations associated with the Fourth Industrial Revolution – is crammed with 'managers of the future'. The men-like-gods hubris is nothing new, but the tech-heroes of the twenty-first century have unprecedented power to pursue a seemingly rational and benign, yet potentially perilous, scenario of remodelling imperfect humans into happy Frankenstein monsters (Bostrom, 2019; Harari, 2016).

4 Happiness from an Evolutionary Perspective

Evolutionary contributions to the field of happiness studies got under way in the 2000s (Diener, 2009c). Prosperous countries in the West have idealized happiness, but some well-being scholars argued that there are both potential benefits of feeling unhappy and downsides to feeling happy. Suarez and Gallup (1985) hypothesized that that depression could be a response to reproductive failure. Andrews and Thomson (2009) explored how depression could be an adaptation that helped our ancestors analyse complex problems. Psychic suffering may trigger deep reflection and psychomotor changes that reduce exposure to distracting stimuli. Andrews and Thomson suggest that because complex analysis is time-consuming, being immobilized by a depressive state could help the afflicted gain insight into how to address challenges or solve problems.

In our ancestral environment, depression could have compelled people to adopt a slow approach to problem-solving and to forge endurance and acceptance of their predicament (Gruber et al., 2011). In the modern context, drugs and distractions allow us to temporarily reduce psychological pain without solving the underlying problem. The question is whether treating depression as a disorder can prevent us from undergoing the learning process which our ancestors had little choice but to submit to.[16]

Gruber et al. have also applied a critical approach to happiness, suggesting when and how it could be dysfunctional. We can (1) be too happy, (2) be happy at the wrong time, (3) pursue happiness in wrong ways, and (4) experience the wrong types of happiness. These generalized hypotheses need further substantiation and exemplification. The work of Gruber et al. was not anchored in the evolutionary sciences but pointed to limitations in how scholars had conceptualized well-being. Perhaps happiness should not always be thought of as something that should be maximized.

Oishi et al. (2009) found that the search for positive affect through novel experiences, like switching partners and chasing ever-new and stronger stimuli, often led to instability in a person's life. There exists a rich folklore about the 'happiest people in the world' – film stars, musicians, influencers – which shows that pressures to radiate glamour and success can give rise to risky behaviour and drug abuse. Such pressures seem to affect more and more people in today's world of social media. The misunderstood imperative to be happy and successful, to flaunt a smiling face to the world, has become a part of the 'digital self' of the young generation. For influencers, a happy exterior is part of the branding and advertising that creates the perception of success. Research shows that behind such designer selves there is often a reality of growing anxiety, fear, and confusion which wrecks many lives and careers. We will return to these modern threats to well-being in Section 5.2.

4.1 An Evolutionary Recipe for a Fulfilling Life

Since our well-being system rewards success related to individual selection with a *positional bias* – that is, in a relative manner – who we view as our comparison group is of crucial importance. Our forager ancestors compared themselves to a few dozen in-group members, a couple of hundred at the most. Individuals competed for a dozen or two potential mates.

---

[16] A qualification is in order. There are cases of severe depression or post-traumatic stress disorder which no dose of learning can eliminate or assuage. An outright rejection of modern remedies that make people's lives more livable overlooks cases where such drugs can not just stimulate creativity, but enhance acceptance of terminal conditions or alleviate grief; see Pollen (2018).

For agriculturalists, too, small comparison groups were the norm until modern times. Cities give us thousands of other individuals to compete against and select between. Mass media exposes us to the successes of people we will never meet, but whose luxury goods, high-value partners, and exciting lifestyles we can learn of in painstaking detail. Social media lets us covet the successes of the world's most accomplished people. Our comparison group can now comprise billions.

Envy motivated our ancestors to try harder to match their neighbours' achievements. Many succeeded. Today, 99+ per cent of people have a miniscule chance of becoming glamorous billionaires with tens of millions of social media followers. With the bar raised sky high, envy and depression can throw us into bottomless pits of despair rather than be a helpful kick in the butt. As mentioned earlier, social media – which can be an arena of compulsive comparisons and the narcissistic focus on the self – seems to explain, at least in part, the past decade's rise in youth depression (Foa & Mounk, 2019; Hellevik & Hellevik, 2021).

Cultivating an attitude of gratitude can function as an antidote to comparing ourselves to more successful individuals. By being grateful for what we already have, we shift focus from our comparison group – and from what we lack – to what we can cherish and what makes us unique (Emmons & McCallough, 2003).[17] Receiving gratitude can have a similar effect. Our inherent positional bias can be modified by engaging in altruistic activities. Volunteering often involves interaction with people who are worse off than ourselves. Research shows that being confronted with the suffering of others can make altruists recalibrate their comparison group in a manner that generates greater well-being (Strack et al., 1990). According to Hill and Buss (2008), people could increase their well-being through reducing their exposure to comparison-inducing media and relaxing their fixation on high-performing individuals.

As argued earlier, many ancient sources and modern positive psychologists agree that happiness is not a destination point. It is a journey. It is an intermittent reward that tells us that we are making solid progress. Theoretically, the secret of a happy life is to make gradual progress, reaching as high as we can, maintaining modest goals. Nesse emphasizes the considerable influence people have on their own well-being through interpreting events and negotiating expectations. Psychological dispositions can drive ill-being, but so do ambitions. A key to happiness is to choose ambitions that match your talents. If you pride yourself on being overly ambitious in life, you may achieve more, but the

---

[17] Emmons and McCullough define gratitude as a two-step process: (1) 'recognizing that one has obtained a positive outcome' and (2) 'recognizing that there is an external source for this positive outcome'.

price you are likely to pay is increased ill-being. If you adjust your goals so that they better match your talents and resources, you will probably feel better. Life is good, writes Nesse (2005),

> when there are sufficient time, energy, and resources to successfully pursue current goals . . . What really counts is the viability of the overall motivational structure, that is, the degree to which all major goals can be pursued success-fully without unduly compromising others. If this is correct, it means that survey studies of well-being will overlook most of what is important.

4.2 A Multilevel Selection Model for Well-Being

This section of the Element – inspired by works cited earlier – originated as a response to Buss and Nesse's calls for an evolutionary approach to well-being (Buss, 2000; Hill & Buss, 2008; Nesse, 2005). Combining their studies of happiness with Baumeister's work on meaning allows us to synthesize the insights of the well-being field under an umbrella of multilevel selection (MLS). The MLS perspective highlights how human evolution has occurred under two often-conflicting pres-sures: individual and group selection. Individuals are incentivized to be selfish to outcompete in-group members. Yet the fact that that group members also had to pull in the same direction was crucial throughout the genus *Homo*'s evolutionary past, which was marked by inter-group competition and war. These insights were summed up by David Sloan Wilson and Edward O. Wilson in a now-famous aphorism: 'Selfishness beats altruism within groups. Altruistic groups beat selfish groups. Everything else is commentary' (2007: 46).

We propose that it can be profitable to think of human well-being as having evolved to affectively motivate individuals to contribute to their own success and that of their group. If we approached happiness and meaning as unconnected, we would overlook how sensations of well-being help individuals manoeuvre between the potentially conflicting pressures of individual and group selection. We sum up our approach with the following equation: 'Happiness + Meaning = Well-Being'.

The terms 'happiness' and 'meaning' are used with a variety of definitions in scholarly and popular contexts. As argued earlier, as concepts, they have different connotations depending on language and culture. Within positive psychology, there has been considerable discussion around which specific affects contribute to happiness as opposed to pride, satisfaction, meaning, and other proposed compo-nents of well-being. Our model is agnostic in this regard. We do not consider it fruitful to try to compile lists of affects that should be associated with happiness and meaning, respectively. Such lists would vary between cultures. Moreover, a multitude of semantic disagreements over how certain terms for affects should be understood has little explanatory value. In line with our MLS model, 'happiness' can be defined as comprising the cluster of affects that promotes individual selection. 'Meaning', on the other hand, can be taken as referring to an amalgam of emotions and cognitions that promote group selection.

There is considerable overlap between the happiness and meaning clusters. Winning in-group contests can be experienced as living up to cultural ideals. Quite often, we solve adaptively relevant challenges for ourselves while also contributing to our group. The biocultural mechanisms of this well-being system are far too complex to untangle, as are its specific sources. Happiness has a stronger biological foundation, but it cannot be accessed without cultural mediation. Meaning is predominantly cultural, but it is made possible by universal predispositions (Baumeister et al., 2013; Ricard, 2015).

Precisely which affects motivate people to different actions is outside the purview of our model. To understand how sensations of well-being propel adaptation on individual and group levels, we need not philosophize with regard to what well-being should be or which affects or virtues it consists of. Nature and culture have already negotiated this content within each individual, group, and moral community – with varying degrees of functionality. Understanding how a distinct culture motivates certain behaviours with regard to meaning and happiness calls for deep insights into a community's history. But from our MLS perspective, to comprehend well-being itself we need not opine on ontology and semantics, a practice that is inevitably culturally biased. It is sufficient to view well-being as a biocultural phenomenon that makes people feel 'good' – or 'right' – in a manner that motivates them to continue the behaviour that has generated well-being.

We cannot expect the well-being system to function precisely and consistently. It will not always trigger an adaptive response. Evolution shaped our affects so that they should, on average, motivate behaviours that tend to maximize reproductive success (Nesse, 2005). Emotions will regularly arise from misunderstandings or motivate a dysfunctional response. In the modern world, environmental mismatch further undermines the precision of our emotional responses. Our MLS approach therefore cannot prescribe in detail how to make populations or individuals flourish, nor can any other perspective on well-being. People and their communities are far too complex and diverse. Understanding sensations of well-being as contributing to multilevel selection has theoretical value, but our model's practical utility comes from combining the MLS perspective with Wilson's work on prosociality (Atkins et al., 2019; Wilson, 2015). This fusion lets us illuminate the distinction between the two forms of social behaviour: competitive and cooperative/prosocial (Figure 1).

While cooperation is a win-win behaviour, prosocial acts can also be altruistic, that is, win-intentional lose (competitive behaviour is win-lose). *Oxford Reference* defines 'prosocial behaviour' as helping others, altruism, or acts

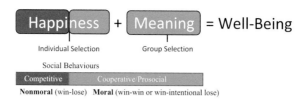

Figure 1 This multilevel selection model for well-being attempts to remedy positive psychology's Western-centrism and conceptual overabundance while drawing attention to the more accessible, prosocial aspects of enhancing the quality of life. Happiness pursuits can be both competitive *and* prosocial. Successful meaning pursuits are prosocial, that is, beneficial for all involved.

meant to promote the interests of society. Figure 1 illustrates how human well-being is derived from competitive (red) and prosocial (green) sources. Meaning quests are prosocial, as their actions are designed to directly benefit others. In spite of altruism being conceptualized as win-intentional lose, the altruist typically receives affective rewards and can make gains as an individual in an indirect way (reproductive, reputational, etc.). Happiness quests can involve both competitive and prosocial behaviours. Solving adaptively relevant challenges benefits the individual, but because humans are a social species, we regularly cooperate with allies to achieve individual goals.

The adaptive benefit of sociality (Lewis et al., 2015), as well as indirect fitness concerns (centred on family and kin), allows us to reap happiness from spending time with our immediate circles of family and friends, and also helping them with and appreciating their accomplishments. Such activities are conceptualized as non-competitive sources of well-being. For many people, the most accessible happiness derives from the adaptive functions of mating, friendship, kinship, and coalition (Buss, 2000). Compared to in-group competition, investing in these activities is more likely to pay off in terms of a higher quality of life. Naturally, individuals cannot opt out of solving important adaptive challenges. But when strategizing as to how to use one's resources to improve personal well-being, it can be the wiser choice to focus on the prosocial mainsprings of human flourishing, such as being social and working for the benefit of others.

4.3 Problematizing Meaning

Baumeister (Baumeister, 2005; Baumeister et al., 2013) conceptualizes happiness and meaning in a similar way to how we do in our model, but he does not invoke the multilevel selection framework. Instead of viewing partially discordant demands for individual and group success as evolutionary pressures that must be navigated, he offers a moral distinction. He connects meaning and happiness, respectively, to giving and taking. When we compete as individuals, our gains are often at the expense of others. When we contribute altruistically, we give to members of our community, a practice which Baumeister values higher than competition.

Animals are mostly incentivized to help kin. Warneken and Tomasello (2009) place the roots of human altruism – in the form of instrumental helping – with our common human ancestry with chimpanzees. Yet chimp prosociality mostly limits itself to close kin, small hunting groups, and boundary enlargement. Other social behaviours tend to be highly competitive; chimps seem not to care much for the well-being of non-kin (Silk et al., 2005; Wrangham, 2019a, 2019b). With the evolution of imaginative culture – around 70,000 years ago (Bellah, 2011; Dawkins & Wong, 2016; Harari, 2014)[18] – *Homo sapiens* became able to extend natural predispositions for nurture to non-kin, and even strangers.

Expanding our in-groups to include groups of non-kin was a great evolutionary leap (Wilson, 2007). Such prosociality, boosted by cultural norms and ideals, made large-scale sociality possible. Human groups would not have been able to grow beyond our species' Dunbar number of around 150 interpersonal relationships if culture did not facilitate impersonal prosociality. We would have remained an insignificant ape (Harari, 2014). Our capacity for meaning allowed us to override self-interest, writes Baumeister (2005: 135), as 'nature makes each creature selfish, but culture functions best if people will sometimes set aside their selfish wishes and impulses in order to do what is best for everyone, that is, for the collective'.

Our ancestors' newfound capacity for uniting around cultural values facilitated prosociality by turning what benefits the group into intrinsic motivation for members via our well-being system. Because we want to feel good, we are driven to do what cultural scripts compel us to do, as this is emotionally rewarding. The well-being we can derive from meaning pursuits can be much greater – and longer lasting – than happiness pursuits can offer. Individuals can be convinced to entirely disregard their own fitness. Self-sacrificing soldiers and suicide bombers exemplify how culture can trigger such intense affect that individuals become *devoted actors* who eagerly sacrifice their lives for their group and its abstract values (Atran et al., 2014). Their reward is being suffused by a deep sense of meaning in this act of self-immolation. The evolutionary rationale behind such overwhelming experiences seems to be to impel individuals to place group needs first.

---

[18] Bellah (2011) places the emergence of imaginative culture 60,000–80,000 years ago. Harari (2014) suggests 70,000 years. Dawkins and Wong (2016) point to 50,000 years. *Homo sapiens'* creative revolution could also have been a more drawn-out affair with older origins.

The potency of meaning is closely related to the feeling of self-esteem, which is a crucial component of well-being (Kirkpatrick & Navarrete, 2010; Solomon et al., 2000). Well-socialized people feel good about themselves to the extent that they live up to cultural ideals. When in-group members put us in higher esteem, we experience our elevation as gratifying. When they look less favourably on us, we are distressed. Self-esteem is adaptive because it results from, and reinforces, social belonging, which offers powerful advantages in terms of survival and reproduction (Baumeister, 2005).

As our communities grew from dozens, to hundreds, to thousands, to millions of individuals, our ancestors had to craft new forms of cooperation that motivated large-scale buy-in. To make people tie their destiny to larger numbers, they expanded their circles of prosociality. Darwin (1871) considered this to be 'the noblest part of our nature'. He stressed *Homo sapiens*' ability to extend our nurturing instinct to larger circles, from offspring and kin to social groups, and nations, and even other species. When some modern humans are able to view humanity itself as their in-group, they can derive meaning – and thus well-being – from helping faceless strangers in far-away places.

Baumeister draws a temporal axis for how meaning functions differently to happiness. Happiness relates to our wants and needs in the present. Meaning integrates our past with the present and future. We interpret our experiences in the light of cultural values. If we can understand our past in a way that empowers us with regard to the future, past distress – or even trauma – can be infused with meaning. If we anchor our present-day actions in an imagined value-charged future outcome, what we do feels meaningful. The longer the timescale, the deeper the sense of meaning. This mechanism can motivate enormous sacrifices for a utopian community that lies decades – or generations – ahead, or in the afterlife.

Meaning pursuits can also turn dysfunctional, even extremely so. It may feel deeply meaningful to submit to a radical political ideology, a religious sect, or another creed. 'Altruistic pathologies' underpinned many of humanity's greatest follies and atrocities. Similar to the ways in which the pursuit of happiness through individual success can be taken too far – to individual and communal detriment – pursuing meaning through personal sacrifice has the potential to ruin lives. In their work on pathologies of altruism, Oakley et al. (2011) examine an array of domains in which our meaning system can become corrupted and lead the altruist astray.

Baumeister does not focus on these potential pitfalls. He takes a normative stand for meaning over happiness, concluding that

> people who sacrifice their personal pleasures in order to participate constructively in society may make substantial contributions. Cultivating and encouraging such people despite their unhappiness could be a goal worthy of

positive psychology . . . Happiness without meaning characterizes a relatively shallow, self-absorbed, or even selfish life, in which things go well, needs and desires are easily satisfied and difficult or taxing entanglements are avoided . . . The meaningful but unhappy life is in some ways more admirable than the happy but meaningless one. (Baumeister, 2013: 515–16)

4.4 Happiness + Meaning = Well-Being

Quantitative studies establish valuable correlations between life factors but fall short of explaining these mechanisms at a deeper level (Hui et al., 2020; Moche & Västfjäll, 2021). Experimenting has been of limited utility in this pursuit (Charness & Grosskopf, 2001; Konow & Earley, 2002). Meier and Stutzer (2008) explain the suboptimal outcome of laboratory studies by how such stimuli provide too meagre stakes to influence reported life satisfaction. Our MLS model advances an approach to the connection between prosociality and individual and social flourishing which offers several advantages. First, it makes a distinction between happiness and meaning in order to highlight different functions of individual and group selection in forging human well-being. Second, it relies on a synergy of quantitative, qualitative, and historically based studies. Third, it attempts to flesh out both cultural and universal elements of human well-being.

In this section, we will illustrate the workings of our MLS model through a study we conducted in 2022, in the aftermath of Putin's invasion of Ukraine (Larsen & Witoszek, 2023; Larsen et al., 2023). The informants in our qualitative study were volunteers ($n = 32$) who helped Ukrainian refugees in Norway. By selecting dedicated altruists, we gained access to thick descriptions of prosocial motivation and experience. The collected insights let us examine the specifics of the human well-being system. Our main concern was to understand the ways in which altruistic activities contribute to the well-being of culturally diverse volunteers. Can we talk about cultural varieties of altruism as practiced by Polish, Russian, Ukrainian, and Norwegian helpers? What narratives, root metaphors, and images did they use to communicate their experiences?

Many Polish volunteers felt that the Ukrainian war was also *their* war, so that they had a particular responsibility to contribute. Their strong engagement infused their lives with meaning, guiding their actions during a difficult time, and sending them off on an exciting, though unpredictable, journey. Many informants felt empowered, expanded their social circles, experienced personal growth, and became eager to advocate the benefits of altruism. A Ukrainian woman said, 'What is happening to me now is like a whole new life. I was someone who could not make any decisions on their own or fix things. I needed help. But not anymore. I feel like I'm bigger on the inside, that I have room for more people.'

Experiencing altruistic reward, several Slavonic informants bemoaned how volunteering had atrophied in their native countries. A Ukrainian man said, 'Working together is the only way to build trust. For now, in Russia and Ukraine, people generally do not trust the government, police, doctors – it's a sad life.' A Belarusian man said, 'We fear scams, spies, propaganda. We want to help, but we have to focus on our own house. I cannot tell my friends in Belarus that I do voluntary work now. They would think I was a political activist only out to please the party to earn money for myself.'

Meaning-generating activities do not necessarily trigger positive affect in the present (Dakin et al., 2021). Certain forms of altruism do produce moments of elation, but meaning seems, to a greater extent than happiness, to induce a lasting sense of well-being. Often, this is more a process than a moment. Such a process can involve a slow recognition of one's own potential and sometimes a discovery of hidden talents. Many of our Slavonic informants reported feeling distressed and emotionally drained due to identification with the war's victims. In the long run, however, they experienced a more persisting sense of purpose and sense to their lives. 'Nothing is more meaningful than helping others to restore their dignity and humanity,' as Polish volunteer Aleksandra put it.

The Belarusian informant wanted his volunteering to benefit his new and former community. Slavonic nations should copy Nordic practices to receive similar advantages, he suggested: 'Norwegians are very naïve, thinking everyone is honest like them. But we must choose to be optimistic about the future, we must risk being naïve. We are all in the same boat. A good future requires that we cooperate. I have a 100-year perspective on helping. I want a better world for my children.'

One of the intriguing findings in our project had to do with different, culturally determined styles and strategies of altruism. The Norwegian helpers followed bureaucratic rules and acted in accordance with the official aid codex. Slavonic volunteers tended to work around the system, operated at breakneck speed, and initiated projects that defied existing protocols. It may well be that the Slavonic informants – with their history of anti-communist and anti-state ethos – were motivated by what we term *anti-systemic altruism*, that is, being a good person who challenges an oppressive system. This ethos highlights spontaneity, improvisation, and frequent rule-breaking. In contrast, Norwegian *systemic altruism* has always been based on trust, efficacy, and compliance with institutional requirements.

These cultural differences notwithstanding, for most informants, helping the Ukrainian refugees was more than a feel-good experience. It was often a transformative process which made them discover their hidden potential, even reclaim self-respect. As Polish volunteer Hanna put it:

> I am not an activist, so before I started helping refugees, I went through the classic phases: first scepticism, then amazement, because I did a lot more than I planned, then the excitement of working with others and realizing that I'm changing someone's life for the better, and finally the feeling of creating my own better self in a previously empty space. In the local community, I'm no longer Hanna the wife of the Polish doctor, a mother of three children, and a good wife. I'm Hanna the organizer, a public person. My well-being is related to family for sure, but there are these peaks that only extra-family functions can give you.

These qualitative interviews illuminate aspects of our well-being system that an MLS perspective helps make sense of. As individuals, we are doomed to strive in status contests, but our communities are also dependent on our altruistic contributions. Experiences of happiness and meaning help us respond to these contradictory pressures and navigate between them.

One key to the relative success of Nordic prosociality is aligning what benefits the individual with what strengthens the community. Several informants stressed how Nordic egalitarianism, in combination with jobs that impart a sense of communal contribution, was important for their high quality of life. When success at work also feels like altruism, the result is an amalgam of happiness and meaning, which has an amplifying effect on long-term well-being. For those without such professional positions, and for many retirees, volunteering infuses their lives with meaning and significantly enhances their quality of life. Several informants reported developing a reservoir of meaning to draw well-being from during times when it is harder to achieve happiness.

Since the happiness side of our equation is mostly relative, policy aimed at enhancing meaning has the greatest potential for increasing societal well-being – especially in prosperous countries, in which people's basic material needs have been covered. This conclusion is supported by studies that attest to an intriguing trade-off between happiness and meaning. Some global surveys show that when GDP per capita goes up, on average, happiness increases at almost the exact same rate that meaning diminishes (Oishi & Diener, 2014). One possible explanation behind this relationship could be that when nations do better economically, communal need diminishes, reducing people's access to meaning-providing activities.

This remarkable stability speaks to the relative nature of our well-being. Still, variance between cultures attests to how some environments, like the Nordic ones, are systemically programmed to enhance human flourishing. After gaining happiness from economic growth, finding new ways to promote activities that generate meaning seems to be the most productive way forward. The central role that helping refugees now has among a growing number of

Norwegian voluntary groups lends support to the claim that Norwegians draw part of their high well-being from looking after exceptionally disadvantaged groups. Research substantiates that exposure to those who are worse off makes people appreciate their own life more (Strack et al., 1990). Our MLS perspective illuminates why such dynamics can make volunteering a win-win activity, for the beneficiary, the altruist, and the community as a whole.

5 From Welfare to Well-Being Society: the Nordic Blueprint

The Nordic Model embodies equality, freedom, welfare, and justice, combining these drivers of well-being with great affluence. Norway, Sweden, Finland, Iceland, and Denmark have a rich tradition of peaceful, reform-oriented, and emancipatory politics, as well as a generous welfare system and an identity based on a partnership with nature. In the eyes of many outside observers, since the end of the twentieth century, the Nordics have been the epitome of good governance, environmental concern, and enlightened altruism.

Their ethos is symbolically and politically linked to 'positive development', as evinced by philosopher Arne Næss' Deep Ecology, the Brundtland Commission's idea of 'sustainable development', and massive aid projects in developing countries. Norway uses more than 1 per cent of its GDP on development aid to advance the causes of peace, human rights, and democracy. Nordic social and political programmes represent a visionary energy and a philosophy of pragmatism that undergird perceptions of the welfare state as a *people's home*, one which does not leave anybody behind.[19] Many citizens – including, as we document in Section 5.2, young people who face new challenges – understand their societies as close to reaching a state of *eudaimonia*: an elevated condition of human flourishing.

The path to the Nordic well-being society is a result of many cultural, economic, and geopolitical factors (Larsen, 2021, 2022; Witoszek & Midttun, 2018). From an evolutionary point of view, scale, size, and the dominant cultural ethos have been important. Wilson and Dag Hessen argue,

> Norway functions exceptionally well as a nation. Although it is small in comparison with the largest nations, it is still many orders of magnitude larger than the village-sized groups of our ancestral past. Seen through the lens of evolutionary theory, the dividing line between function and dysfunction has

---

[19] The term 'People's Home' is ascribed to Albin Hansson, the Swedish social-democratic prime minister who used it in a speech in 1928. The metaphor was to transform the Swedes from atomized citizens into members of a social-democratic family united around a common project. As has been shown, the concept of a 'People's Home' has longer roots and was used by the great Swedish writer Selma Lagerlöf at a Women's Congress in 1915; see Witoszek and Sørensen (2018).

been notched upward so that the whole nation functions like a single organism. This is an exaggeration, of course. Self-serving activities that are bad for the group can be found in Norway, but they are modest in comparison with the more dysfunctional nations of the world. Our hypothesis [is that] Norway functions well as a nation because it has successfully managed to scale up the social control mechanisms that operate spontaneously in village-sized groups.[20]

Informed by the global embrace of well-being metrics, Scandinavian societies in the 2010s moved towards redesigning their vision of a good society by emphasizing high quality of life rather than focusing predominantly on economic concerns. We conceptualize this process as a transition from being materialistically oriented welfare societies to becoming more holistic well-being societies. A Norwegian 2022 government White Paper declared,

> We want a society where as many people as possible experience a good quality of life. A strategy for quality of life gives us the basis for effective measures that match the needs of the citizens … We will develop political measures in line with what the citizens emphasize for their quality of life. A good quality of life is about feeling good and functioning well. This is how we want as many people as possible to have it … In measures of quality of life, factors such as health, social relations, working environment or student environment, living conditions, and the experience of social conditions are included. Belonging to a community also brings happiness and increases the quality of life. We know that severe loneliness is linked to a major loss of quality of life. Increased knowledge about the importance of different life conditions for quality of life gives us better knowledge about which actions can have the greatest effect.[21]

5.1 Nature as a Space of Renewal

There is yet another important factor behind high levels of well-being in the Nordic countries: access to – and interaction with – pristine nature, our evolutionary habitat. Scandinavian nature is not just about the ecological environment; it is linked to an array of practices and values based on interaction between humans and the natural world. The most significant Norwegian icons, narratives, and rites – which have empowered and cemented the national community over time –include images, stories, and modes of conduct related to nature (Anker, 2022; Larsen, 2023; Reed & Rothenberg, 1992; Witoszek, 2011).

---

[20] https://davidsloanwilson.world/online-content/blueprint-for-the-global-village-with-dag-hes sen/.

[21] www.regjeringen.no/no/aktuelt/regjeringa-vil-forankre-ein-nasjonal-strategi-for-livskvalitet-i-folkehelsemeldinga/id2947291/.

From Norse poetry to Næss' eco-philosophy, nature has been deployed as a locus of belonging and an emblem of national identity. There is a remarkable consistency in the way nature-inspired tropes and images have been linked to projects which have advanced social justice, equality, peace, and cooperation. Studies on the origins of social democracy point to how the older generations that built 'Happy Norway' had their identity anchored in nature as an ancestral home, the sacred place to regenerate, to cultivate friendship, and to carry out projects requiring collective mobilization for the welfare of others.

In most Nordic cultures, nature use has been a social glue cementing trust between diverse social groups. A variety of activities – from the obligatory Sunday hiking tour, to long visits at summer and winter cottages, and cross-country skiing – have nourished national health, longevity, and well-being. Until recently, Norwegian happiness was intimately connected to the open air, or joys and rituals of *friluftsliv*. In spite of the growing indignation about the Norwegian oil industry as one of the planet's largest polluters, most Norwegians have embraced a cognitive dissonance that allows them to combine their high ecological footprint with their ideal of a good life linked to the idyll of nature. They did so en masse until the second decade of the twenty-first century when new technology and culture brought new challenges (see Section 5.2).

Two additional elements are inherent in modern Nordic well-being societies. First, the idea of self-realization fully extends to all genders. Nordic productivity is in part due to having one of the highest female employment rates (Witoszek & Midttun, 2018). The cultural ideal of gender partnership rather than power struggle or *machismo* accounts for increased well-being for women and men alike. Unlike the more liberal Anglo-Saxon feminism, which is more centred on the individual self, the Nordic model educates men and women to value partnership and teamwork, which affects relationships at home, at the workplace, and in civil society.

The Nordic well-being society is not underpinned merely by economic and political concerns. It is supported by a whole happiness lexicon consisting of words and memes like the Danish *hygge*, the Norwegian *kos*, and the Swedish *lagom* – to mention the most popular examples. These concepts have no exact translations in English, but evoke coziness, harmony, balance, security, and at-homeness in the world – not grandeur or splendour but *kos*; no drama, just de-stressing at a relaxed pace. Or Swedish *lagom*, meaning just the right amount, not too much or too little.

Implicit in *hygge* or *kos* is the idea that human well-being is not just about relaxing after winning a palatial place with a pool and a Jaguar parked in the garage. *Kos* and *hygge* are about relishing simple pleasures which have little or nothing to do with material gains. For instance, in Norway, the intense experience of *kos* can refer to touchingly trivial pursuits, like rewarding oneself with a piece of chocolate, a biscuit, or an orange after climbing to the top of a slope. Little matches the calm ecstasy of sitting atop a mountain with a magnificent view, and slowly peeling one's well-deserved orange.

Policy-wise, to promote the community of *kos*, one could aim for shorter work weeks, longer vacations, and subsidized day care, as well as investment in arenas that enable people to come together to solve concrete tasks of communal importance – like building a new playground – or just to enjoy each other's company.

The Nordics exemplify our model of well-being as an amalgam of happiness and meaning. While accepting that there are many paths to individual self-realization, Nordic culture promotes a model of education, and a *Bildung*, which associates well-being with humanitarian projects at home and abroad. For the regular Scandinavian, life becomes imbued with meaning when individual happiness is linked to work for the common good and helping the needy, wherever they may be.

5.2 The Nordic Model under Siege: Twenty-First-Century Challenges to Human Flourishing

Several intriguing – if not disturbing – features of the transition of Norway to a well-being society have been signalled by international indexes and national research findings. From 2018 to 2023, Norway fell from being the happiest society in the *World Happiness Report* to number 7. The cause seems primarily to be a marked decrease of well-being among the young.

In surveys from the 1980s on, 15- to 24-year-olds were mostly the happiest while the oldest generation were the least happy. In the period 2009–2019, this relationship was inverted (Hellevik & Hellevik, 2021). The Norwegian Monitor's quantitative study concluded that the main sources of youth ill-being were loneliness, dissatisfaction with health and physical fitness, poor relationships with family and friends, dissatisfaction with gender equality, worries about the future, and high levels of stress related to the imperative to succeed and excel.

Our own qualitative interviews with high school students point to excessive use of social media as an important source of reduced well-being. In terms of cultural evolution, a new development seems to be underway. Sherry Turkle (2012) argues that curating one's online profiles alters the presentation of the self and, ultimately, influences individual identity. The ethos 'I share, therefore I am' drives people to craft their identities for others. Continuous digital performance, even if successful, often leads to disconnection anxiety or a 'fear of missing out', so-called FOMO.

The compulsion to compare oneself with others is a source of stress and anxiety. The have-nots suffer because they do not live up to their ideals and aspirations, while the haves suffer because of a pressure to match the have-mores.

Facebook and TikTok facilitate a commodification of individual identity, incentivizing the young to present themselves as living happy, enviable lives. Paradoxically, for many young captives of the vicarious life through social media, our era's 'ideology of well-being' results in greater ill-being.

Adding to the misery of the young is a growing disconnection from nature. Unlike for their parents and grandparents, *friluftsliv* – the ideal of regenerative communing with fjords, forests, and mountains – seems to have lost much of its appeal to the young generation. Gym workouts give quicker and more visible results than walking or skiing. Hiking in the forest or going to a summer cottage is now surveyed through the eye of Instagram and distracted by a stream of messages flowing from social media.

It is too early to conclude what consequences the ongoing digitalization and 'nature deficit disorder' will entail for the young members of well-being societies. What is certain is that the twenty-first-century youth will have to cope with the unpredictable sociopolitical, economic – as well as evolutionary – challenges pertaining to the age of 'dataism' (Harari, 2016).

6 Conclusions

An MLS perspective offers no magic recipe for forging well-being societies, but our model's emphasis on prosociality provides some guidance. It would be unfortunate if the Western obsession with happiness pursuits led to an even higher level of competition between members of the same national community. The United States – a country which has been a modern theatre of the gladiatorial struggle of egos and a monomanic focus on selfish aspirations – is an example of how a misconceived survival of the fittest can increase inequality and undermine democracy.

Striking the right balance between individualism and communitarianism is key. The challenge is to develop cultural values and institutions that facilitate a greater focus on cooperative practices and a prosocial ethos. A better understanding of how human nature interacts with cultural legacy can be of great benefit to such a process. Mechanically adopting wholesale solutions from nations with significantly different norms and practices is rarely workable, though models of good society could serve as valuable inspiration.

There are many voices – some of them coming from the ecological frontier – that call for dropping the fetish of economic growth. In 2018, 238 scientists called on the European Commission to abandon GDP growth and focus on human well-being and ecological stability instead.[22] In a report, *Mismeasuring*

---

[22] www.theguardian.com/politics/2018/sep/16/the-eu-needs-a-stability-and-wellbeing-pact-not-more-growth.

Our Lives (2008), the Nobel Prize winners in economics, Amartya Sen and Joseph Stiglitz, show the limits of GDP as a measurement of social well-being.[23] Not only does GDP overlook economic inequality (with the result that most people can be worse off, even though average income is increasing); it fails to factor in environmental impacts into economic decisions that, in turn, affect the well-being of humans and their environment. In the bestseller *Less Is More: How Degrowth Will Save the World* (2020), Jason Hickel proposes a radical re-organizing of Western economies around well-being rather than capital accumulation. Degrowth, he argues, does not need to lead to a more Puritan world. On the contrary, the ethos of degrowth is to create a world where pleasure, fun, and conviviality would reign supreme.

That said, many experts consider degrowth and reducing competition as a challenging – some would say utopian – agenda.[24] The question is: how utopian are they? The Nordic nations are an interesting case in this regard, as they are prosocial without discarding competition. As we argued, their altruistic *Bildung* has deep cultural roots and is hard to emulate by countries with different histories. But allocating more resources to cooperative pursuits and work for the common good is possible even in individualistic, competitive cultures such as the United States. Hurricane Katrina, which tore over New Orleans in 2005, led to an explosion of altruistic behaviour in the affected population. Rutger Bregman argues that crisis brings out not the worst but the best in the American people (2020: 4–6). And, paradoxically, in spite of its legendary individualism (Hofstede Insights, 2019), the United States also boasts the highest rates of volunteering (Anheier & Salamon, 1999).

American culture has cultivated fierce competition, but also developed a deeply entrenched tradition of individual philanthropy, a legacy that is missing in a country like Norway. An interesting study would be to compare Scandinavian and American wealth-sharing. Highly competitive, or class-ridden societies – such as the United States and the United Kingdom – have developed the tradition of philanthropy which is dependent on a variety of individual motives, whether springing from the feeling of guilt about unequal distribution of resources, inner generosity, or a manipulative strategy to display

---

[23] https://wcfia.harvard.edu/publications/mismeasuring-our-lives-why-gdp-doesnt-add.

[24] Scholarly authorities such as Paul Collier (Gedde-Dahl, 2020) and Noah Smith (2021) have pointed out that degrowth appeals most to privileged people in wealthy countries. Economist Branko Milanović (2017) has argued that achieving reduced growth either means keeping a significant proportion of the world's population in the South in poverty or sharply reducing the income of most people in the North. The former is unacceptable to supporters of low growth, and the latter is politically impossible; see www.morgenbladet.no/ideer/2020/11/27/en-egois tisk-middelklasse-har-sveket-resten-av-samfunnet-mener-paul-collier/, www.noahpinion.blog/ p/people-are-realizing-that-degrowth, and http://glineq.blogspot.com/2017/11/the-illusion-of-degrowth-in-poor-and.html.

one's wealth or attain political influence. In Scandinavian countries, prosociality – although also springing from multiple sources – has been the cumulative result of a cultural habitus, a top-down and bottom-up socialization into altruism combined with state education towards 'do-goodism'.

Our preliminary hypothesis – that American philanthropy may be a form of *ersatz* competition and selfishness – needs corroboration. Whatever the answer, a deeper understanding of cultural values and traditions that underpin human well-being is important. While some human desires are fairly universal, the ways in which they play out in the digital era are complex and require synergic approaches to society based on an interaction between evolutionary science, economy, psychology, and cultural history.

6.1 From Play and Flow to Happiness for Sale

Competing for happiness will always be part of human life. But once the basic adaptive challenges are solved – or when the competitive paths to happiness are less attractive – individuals can be better off pursuing the prosocial sources of well-being. Alas, also these sources can be hard to access in some cultures. The practice of impersonal prosociality can be prohibitively costly in dysfunctional environments. Being overly generous to strangers in highly selfish, low-trust societies is a recipe for being taken advantage of or punished (Balliet & Van Lange, 2013; Gintis, 2008), which tends to reduce well-being. Any form of altruism can be risky, or impossible, in the most oppressive of regimes, such as North Korea. Tyrants and dictators fear prosociality because of its empowering, agency-building capacity. The most spectacular social transformations – from Gandhi's peaceful resistance to the Polish Solidarity movement of the 1980s – were based on the awakening of human altruism and compassion which contributed to the collapse of empires.

There is one more source of well-being which merits attention: the human capacity for play and creativity. *Homo ludens* is a natural hero of the happy, joyful world whose aspects have been studied by Johan Huizinga (2016) and Mihaly Csikszentmihalyi (2008). Huizinga points to play as both universal and autotelic; that is, it has no function beyond eliciting a spirited joy of playfulness in both human and some animal species. But, in the case of humans, the nature of play is often enriched by a creative process that defamiliarizes the familiar and leads to artistic and scientific breakthroughs. Csikszentmihalyi drew attention to the key element of play by deploying the concept of *flow*. He studied the mental state of 'being in the zone' – a peak of enchanted self-transcendence. Being in the flow is entering into a sphere of timelessness in which the ego is partly dissolved and rules feel less like a hindrance and more like an exciting challenge. Playing music, engaging in sport activities, and engaging in spiritual exercise are mentioned as mainsprings of flow. Ludic activities create a world which, at least for a moment, is immune to limitations, existential constraints, and even the trauma of war. Joys of creativity and innovation combine a sense of mastery and enchanted expectations which, in turn, increase happiness and self-realization (Buss, 2000; Csikszentmihalyi, 1997a, 1997b; Haidt, 2006; Seligman, 2000).

The question is: Can we *learn* to be more ludic and creative? Are there any steps to reaching flow – the omega point of happiness? In his bestseller *Happiness: A Guide to Developing Life's Most Important Skill* (2007), Matthieu Ricard argues that happiness can be reached through a process of learning – but not without a price. That is to say, there is a 'happiness codex' to be followed and a skill to be honed for those who can afford to listen to Ricard, standing in his maroon and orange robes among the glitterati of the World Economic Forum in Davos. The sight of the eudaimonic guru may be inspiring to some and unsettling to others. What is inspiring is Ricard's meteoric rise from a modest Buddhist sage to a leader of meditation and happiness sessions for industrial tycoons, Nobel-winning academics, and heads of state. What is unsettling is the realization that there is a 'happiness market' which commodifies our dreams and aspirations.

We live in the age in which the mining, processing, and selling of mass data is not just the fundament of 'surveillance capitalism' (Zuboff, 2018), but the domain of marketeers. There are reasons to fear that soon neuroscience and psychology, in alliance with social economics, will have located happiness, measured it, and made it ready to be sold as part of the growing eudaimonic industry. Some critical commentators predict that the mathematical, mechanized view of the mind will triumph, simply because of the financial rewards of objectively defined happiness. 'Positive psychologists and happiness economists make a great play of the fact that money and material possessions don't lead to an increase in our mental wellbeing,' declares the writer William Davies in *The Guardian*:

> But these experts are in a minority, compared with the vast assemblage of consumer psychologists, consumer neuroscientists and market researchers all dedicated to ensuring that we do achieve some degree of emotional satisfaction by spending money .... Happiness is nailed down to a certain amount of gamma wave activity in the left prefrontal cortex, or a moral decision spurred by an oxytocin surge ... Already many emotions have been 'medicalised' – not, some who work in the field say, in order to help patients, but to sell drugs. (Renton, 2015)

This is a disturbing reflection. While positive psychology, mindfulness, and pharmaceuticals can all potentially be helpful, a covert cultural brainwashing which fetishizes happiness as a must, whatever the cost, is dangerous both to society and to the democratic order as we know it.

6.2 Improving on the MLS Model

The MLS model of human well-being as drafted in this Element invites further work. For well-being scholars, our evolutionary approach can hopefully inspire productive lines of enquiry. To substantiate the utility of an MLS model, our empirical research mostly explored the sources of meaning and their connection to well-being among altruistic volunteers (Larsen & Witoszek, 2023; Larsen et al., 2023). Quantitative studies could shed further light on the array of motivations and inspirations that energize prosocial work. In what ways do other categories of altruistic actors than the ones we interviewed benefit from helping others? More in-depth qualitative studies could illuminate varieties of prosociality in other contexts than voluntary work to help refugees from countries with cultural norms in opposition to prevalent Western metrics and values.

Cross-cultural studies with a wider range than ours should offer fertile contributions to understanding the relationship between human universals and cultural and historical legacies. With regard to expanding one's circles of prosociality, we expect there to be significant variance in scale and narrative justification of altruistic acts. Studying non-WEIRD nations and kinship societies could help us better understand the biocultural influences that inform our criteria for whom to help and what strategies are most effective.

We propose that scholars think flexibly in terms of which group levels an MLS perspective should include. Of particular interest could be the distinction between solving adaptively relevant challenges individualistically or as part of a group (Figure 2). Collaborative activities allow individuals to harvest the diverse rewards related to individual and group selection. Progressing towards goals generates happiness, while aiding other group members offers interpersonal meaning. If this were to occur under mortal threat, *identity fusion* can make individuals feel closer to other group members than to kin (Atran et al., 2014). Individuals who tie their destinies together – especially in challenging or perilous environments – make happiness and meaning merge in a manner that can greatly elevate well-being. There are numerous testimonies from soldiers who, after war, long to go to back to the strongly rewarding affect that their previous group activities generated in situations of intense danger.

How a similar togetherness can be cultivated in modern, peaceful environments is not clear. Intriguingly, well-being studies from cultures that emphasize interdependent flourishing, such as the Confucian ones, report lower well-being

Figure 2 When people form close-knit groups that work to solve everyone's
adaptive challenges, this can have a powerful effect on well-being.
Succeeding in competition against other groups generates happiness.
Reciprocal altruism between members generates meaning from interpersonal
prosociality. The group can draw additional meaning from bestowing
impersonal prosociality upon members of the larger community. Future
research should investigate how best to facilitate activities that let people tap
into multiple sources of well-being.

(Krys et al., 2021b; Rappleye et al., 2020). Is this due to a local preference for
lower emotional intensity? To what extent are these populations influenced by
their existential constraints? Or does peaceful interdependence require that
individuals restrain their emotions so as not to be group outliers?

We justified our equation 'Happiness + Meaning = Well-Being' by emphasizing the importance of viewing the human well-being system as one, affected
by both individual and group selection. There is a need for further investigation
of how psychological and environmental demands affect individual strategies
for well-being. How people prioritize differently between sources of well-being
when facing a crisis could be another productive avenue for further study.
Nesse's hypothesis, that high levels of well-being are a result of adaptive signal
interpretation and goal adjustment, needs further substantiation. Qualitative
research on people who have gone through crisis and goal re-evaluation could
help illuminate the mechanisms of personal and social renewal.

These questions suggest some of the ways in which studies of well-being
could be enriched by a biocultural MLS perspective. How does it affect the
human reward system to raise the primary level of competition from us as
individuals to our social group? Does it feel better to win alone or as a group?
Does failing together feel less bad? What is the difference between meaning
springing from altruistic activities that benefit members of our interpersonally
related social group, and actions that benefit strangers? Is it more rewarding to
engage in altruistic activities alone or as a group?

Figure 2 illustrates how we conceptualize these levels. Individual and social-
group functionality relies on ancient cognitive mechanisms. At the level of the

moral community – today, typically one's nation – we rely on culture (Henrich, 2020). With interpersonal relations, we can, to a great extent, depend on *Homo sapiens'* reflex for reciprocity (Haidt, 2006). To cultivate prosociality among strangers, we need well-functioning norms, values, and institutions. A deeper understanding of how interpersonal altruism, juxtaposed with impersonal altruism, affects our well-being system could be of paramount importance.

There are many themes and methodological tangles that we have only signalled in this Element, and which need further research. Methodologically, exploring the galaxy of 'mongrel concepts' of well-being, happiness, and meaning calls for more in-depth studies comparing what the people say in interviews or questionnaires and what they actually *do*. There is often a gap between words and deeds – a gap which may be a conscious attempt of redesigning the self into a more wished-for specimen, or an unconscious strategy of a 'pilot response' which has not been thought through. Both qualitative and quantitative studies of well-being would also profit from taking into account a dynamic, temporal, and contextual dimension of our perceptions of well-being. These perceptions do not stand still; they change over time and generate conflicting interpretations with regard to not only whether what makes us happy or unhappy in particular situations, but also who we are (or were), and where we are going with our lives.

A possible venue for more exploration has to do with the project of studying and understanding culturally sensitive definitions of well-being. Our biocultural approach is based on the assumption that human beings from all latitudes are biologically wired for harmony and well-being, just as they are wired for the search for freedom and fairness, desire for recognition or altruistic behaviour. It is cultural norms and values, which emphasize particular drives and aspirations, that make us different. The question is: do they – and to what degree?

To mention but one example of a conundrum, most Latin Americans and most Africans cherish their cultural traditions, but, when given a chance, they dream of – and vote with their feet – moving to Western countries which profess values conflicting with their indigenous legacies. Respecting the immigrants' separate paths to development and happiness within Western societies is a huge, and unresolved, challenge in modern migration studies. Our model – emphasizing both biological commonalities and cultural differences – may be helpful in balancing more effective solutions. That said, matters are complicated by highly subjective responses to cultural challenges. Some individuals increase their well-being by embracing Western freedoms, while others refuse to be replanted and demand respect while disrespecting their host societies. It is enough to read the Somalian writer's Ayan Hirshi Ali's biography *Infidel* (2008), to see the contrasting well-being paths of two young sisters from

Somalia who are replanted as immigrants in Germany. While one of them (Ayan) flourishes and spreads wings, the other, appalled and paralysed by excruciating pressures of Western freedoms, falls into deep depression and – paradoxically – dies of the excess of life choices and opportunities that life in the West has to offer.

Ayan Hirshi Ali's story is instructive because – were their contrasting well-being trajectories transposed to the second decade of the twenty-first century – they may have taken a different turn, especially with regard to Ayan's sister. The ongoing virtualization of Western – and immigrants' – lifeworld encourages cultural ghettoization, for better or for worse. Not only it is now possible to happily inhabit in a different culture without speaking its language or comply-ing with 'oppressive' customs of the host country; one can offer one's offspring alternative, home-based models of remote education via internet platforms.

What also needs more research is the role of small groups as triggers or deterrents of individual well-being. On the one hand, our evolutionary past, which goes back to a life in small social groups, programs us to thrive – and effectively solve problems – in intimate settings. The hasty conclusion would be that problems that can be solved at a lower, subsidiary level should be the preferred option than involving a complex machinery. Again, matters are more complicated than that. Many individuals thrive and blossom in small, intimate communities which function as extended families and, at best, as warm circles where everybody feels safe and looked after. But, as we suggested, well-being requires more than the mere satisfying of basic needs or a handful of fleeting moments of happiness. Meaning matters in the equation. The well-being of some inhabitants of local villages is bound to be eroded by a sense of constant surveillance, by strong control mechanisms, or by group pressures on how the proper life should be lived. Cosmopolitan or urban cultures are more relaxed and tolerant of 'deviants', not to mention that they offer a better chance to achieve self-realization and thus increase well-being.

***

Our MLS model does not offer a silver bullet to solve an array of problems bedevilling developed and developing democracies in the twenty-first century. But, as we see it, our MLS approach may have relevance in three key areas which impact social well-being and bear on the design of modern democratic institutions. The first one concerns rethinking of our caring and health services. All too often the well-being of hospital patients is misconceived as dependent on successful surgery or efficient application of medicines. All too frequently patients who have been traumatized or handicapped by serious accidents are treated as cured as soon as they seemingly recover – and left to their own devices. The system is not geared towards attending to their well-being as meaning-making and meaning-seeking individuals. The hazards of progressive bureaucratization of care services are anchored in *increasing efficiency*, not in helping a person to recover a meaningful life. The well-being of patients is a deep black hole in geriatric care, where many patients are treated as travellers at the end of their journey. The widespread misconception is that at this point of their lives, there is no longer any meaning to be found – apart from eating, being put to bed, and occasionally receiving visits from family or friends. If, as our model suggests, meaning is the basis of human well-being, then both the process of recovery of sick patients and the care of the elderly would need to be reimagined by health institutions, social services, and nursing homes.

Second, our biocultural approach to well-being – anchored as it is in cultural sensitivity and universal drives of human nature – has implications for current educational paradigms. Although the Council of Europe talks about 'improving well-being at school',[25] modern educational institutions function mostly as instruments of learning and acquiring knowledge. The discussion of well-being is often reduced to health issues, and there is as yet no project of education to well-being through the pedagogy of meaning-making.

Third, individual and social well-being is often a blind zone in fragile democracies that attempt to rebuild social structures destroyed by despotic or authoritarian regimes. There are other priorities: economic growth, restoring the rule of law, ensuring a minimum welfare. It is easy to forget that stressed and distressed populations are potential victims of authoritarian populists and demagogues. To mention but one example: A country like Poland that regained its democracy in 2023 – after eight years of crypto-fascist rule that specialized in hate and social polarization – faces a demanding project of building a 'democracy 2.0'. Such democracy cannot be reduced to restoring the rule of law and governmental welfare hand-outs that make people 'happy' for a day or two. It has to rely on forging new educational institutions that attend to two often-overlooked projects: (1) a broad emancipative programme that connects meaning with freedom and reclaims individual agency; and (2) a novel pedagogy boosting society's well-being through promoting ideals of altruism and cooperative ethos. The fate of Poland – and of all ailing democracies – is as much dependent on material prosperity as on innovative, meaning-making schooling that emphasizes empowering, can-do stories rather than flaunting a passive-aggressive identity anchored in suffering and hate of the others.

To sum up: more insights into strategies to forge prosociality and cooperation as the condition of human flourishing are vital for rethinking modern democracy

---

[25] www.coe.int/en/web/campaign-free-to-speak-safe-to-learn/improving-well-being-at-school.

and its institutions. As we have indicated earlier, altruism, teamwork, as well as a sense of belonging to a caring community are dependent on close, face-to-face interactions. The age of artificial intelligence, where, increasingly, net-based transactions – from banking to education – has melted the glue that holds communities together. The functioning of e-based institutions may be cheaper, smarter, and more efficient, but the art of building cooperation, friendship, and warmth within families and between generations is eroded. The social bubbles of TikTok, Instagram, and Facebook reduce the imaginative and inspirational energy that flows from people who meet each other in the same physical space.

Although it may sound overambitious, a combination of evolutionary and cultural insights into the drivers of well-being is not just about creating more effective educational and institutional arrangements; it may contribute to humanity's next great evolutionary leap. The twenty-first-century challenge is to craft prosocial culture to solve global problems, from the climate crisis to migration, biological hacking, nuclear proliferation, and artificial intelligence (Bostrom, 2019; Harari, 2016). It has been repeated ad infinitum – by UN leaders,[26] international aid organizations, and scholars – that only cooperation and prosociality can help us address the civilizational crises of our time. For people to expand their circles of empathy to the global level, transnational teamwork and solidarity have to feel good, or at least right and desirable. A synergy between positive psychology and the evolutionary sciences can help policymakers by providing insights into the relationship between impersonal altruism and our well-being system.

In the short run, interdisciplinary insights into the mechanisms of well-being could help counter the ongoing cultural and political polarization which bedevils many societies. Seen most prominently in the United States, reduced impersonal prosociality and an unwillingness to cooperate across political divides diminish political efficacy and undermine social cohesion. This cultural regression results in nationally uniting values and narratives losing their hold. As a sense of belonging to a moral community is reduced, people seem to crave stronger interpersonal relations at a smaller-group level, a process which contributes to what Karl Popper (2020) called the 'retribalization of the world'.

Figure 2 shows how this process entails a devolution of moral allegiance from a higher to a lower level and an intensification of intra-group competition. Societies that turn in on themselves risk being engulfed by political chaos and self-destruction. Evolutionary well-being scholars cannot tell us which values will underpin tomorrow's global village – if one such 'village' comes into being – but they can suggest which values are imperative for preventing social

---

[26] www.un.org/en/common-agenda.

breakdown and ensuring our survival. The search for selfish happiness alone, without the quest for transformative meaning anchored in the prosocial ethos, is pernicious from both an evolutionary and a cultural point of view.

The stakes are significant. Combining insights from contextual, cultural studies, and evolutionary science may guide policymakers in their efforts to improve human cooperation and resilience in crisis situations. Many scientists talk about a 'climate end game', mapping out the potential catastrophes that could follow a 'tipping cascade' and trigger multiple system failures that afflict societies across the globe. Without a social mobilization based on prosociality and cooperation, humanity could face a civilizational collapse. A framework with cross-cultural predictive potential – one that helps those in charge design or reimagine their social and educational policies and evaluate outcomes – could both contribute to improving lives for more people and avert social breakdown in our challenging times.

References

Adler, M. D. (2019). *Measuring Social Welfare: An Introduction*. Oxford University Press. https://doi.org/10.1093/oso/9780190643027.001.0001.

Agarwal, V. (2000). *Hinduism Beyond Ritualism*. Independently published.

Alesina, A., Di Tella, R., & MacCulloch, R. (2004). Inequality and happiness: Are Americans and Europeans different? *Journal of Public Economics*, 88, 2009–42. https://doi.org/10.1016/j.jpubeco.2003.07.006.

Andrews, P. W., & Thomson, J. A. Jr. (2009). The bright side of being blue: Depression as an adaptation for analyzing complex problems. *Psychological Review*, 116(3), 620–54. http://doi:10.1037/a0016242.

Angner, E. (2011). *The Evolution of Eupathics: The Historical Roots of Subjective Measures of Well-Being*. (PhD). University of Alabama at Birmingham. https://doi.org/10.5502/ijw.v1i1.14.

Anheier, H. K., & Salamon, L. M. (1999). Volunteering in cross-national perspective: Initial comparisons. *Law and Contemporary Problems*, 62, 43–65. http://doi.org/10.2307/1192266.

Anker, P. (2022). *Livet er best ute: friluftslivets historie og filosofi*. Kagge forlag.

Arendt, H. (1951). *The Origins of Totalitarianism*. Harcourt, Brace.

Argyle, M. (1999). Causes and correlates of happiness. In D. Kahneman, E. Diener, & N. Schwarz, eds., *Wellbeing: The Foundations of Hedonic Psychology*. Russell Sage Foundation, pp. 353–73.

Atkins, P. W. D., Wilson, D. S., & Hayes, S. C. (2019). *Prosocial: Using Evolutionary Science to Build Productive, Equitable, and Collaborative Groups*. New Harbinger.

Atran, S., Sheikh, H., & Gomez, A. (2014). Devoted actors sacrifice for close comrades and sacred cause. *PNAS*, 111, 17702–3. http://doi.org/10.1073/pnas.1420474111.

Austin, A. (1988). Antitrust reaction to the merger wave: The revolution vs. the counterrevolution. *North Carolina Law Review*, 66(5), 931–62. https://scholarship.law.unc.edu/nclr/vol66/iss5/3.

Austin, A. (2015). On well-being and public policy: Are we capable of questioning the hegemony of happiness? *Social Indicators Research*, 127(1), 1–16. https://doi.org/10.1007/s11205-015-0955-0.

Axelrod, R. (1984). *The Evolution of Cooperation*. Basic Books.

Bacon, F. (1960 [1620]). *The new Organon, and Related Writings*, F. H. Anderson, ed. Liberal Arts Press.

Balliet, D., & Van Lange, P. A. M. (2013). Trust, punishment, and cooperation across 18 societies: A meta-analysis. *Perspectives on Psychological Science*, 8(4), 363–79. http://doi.org/10.1177/1745691613488533.

Bakshi, A. J. (2019). Happiness is not a luxury: Interview with Ed Diener. *British Journal of Guidance & Counselling*, 47(2), 258–62. https://doi.org/10.1080/03069885.2018.1541163.

Baumeister, R. F. (2005). *The Cultural Animal: Human Nature, Meaning, and Social Life*. Oxford University Press. https://doi.org/10.1093/acprof:oso/9780195167030.001.0001.

Baumeister, R. F., Vohs, K. D., Aaker, J. L., & Garbinsky, E. N. (2013). Some key differences between a happy life and a meaningful life. *The Journal of Positive Psychology*, 8(6), 505–16. http://doi.org/10.1080/17439760.2013.830764.

Bellah, R. N. (2011). *Religion in Human Evolution: From the Paleolithic to the Axial Age*. Harvard University Press. https://doi.org/10.4159/harvard.9780674063099.

Bergløff, C. B. (2021). Det nye singelnorge. NRK. www.nrk.no/livsstil/xl/nrk-har-kartlagt-single-i-norge-gjennom-40-ar-1.15685760.

Bhagavad Gita (2007). Trans. E. Easwaran. Nilgiri Press.

Biglan, A., Johansson, M., Ryzin, M. V., & Embry, D. (2020). Scaling up and scaling out: Consilience and the evolution of more nurturing societies. *Clinical Psychology Review*, 81, 101893. http://doi:10.1016/j.cpr.2020.101893.

Block, N. (1995). On a confusion about a function of consciousness. *Behavioral and Brain Sciences*, 18, 227–47. https://doi.org/10.1017/S0140525X00038188.

Bostrom, N. (2019). The vulnerable world hypothesis. *Global Policy*, 10(4), 455–76. http://doi:10.1111/1758-5899.12718.

Bowles, S., & Gintis, H. (2013). *A Cooperative Species: Human Reciprocity and Its Evolution*. Princeton University Press.

Braithwaite, V. A., & Law, H. (1985). Structure of human values: Testing the adequacy of the Rokeach value survey. *Journal of Personality and Social Psychology*, 49(1), 250–63. http://doi.org/10.1037/0022-3514.49.1.250.

Bruner, J. (1990). *Acts of Meaning*. Harvard University Press.

Bruner, J. (1996). *The Culture of Education*. Harvard University Press. https://doi.org/10.4159/9780674251083.

Buchanan, A., & Powell, R. (2018). *The Evolution of Moral Progress: A Biocultural Theory*. Oxford University Press.

Buss, D. M. (1989). Conflict between the sexes: Strategic interference and the evocation of anger and upset. *Journal of Personality and Social Psychology*, 56, 735–47. https://doi.org/10.1037/0022-3514.56.5.735.

Buss, D. M. (2000). The evolution of happiness. *American Psychologist*, 55(1), 15–23. http://doi.org/10.1037/0003-066X.55.1.15.

Buss, D. M. (2003). *Evolution of Desire: Strategies of Human Mating*. Basic Books.

Buss, D. M. (2004). *Evolutionary Psychology: The New Science of the Mind*. Pearson Education.

Chapais, B. (2008). *Primeval Kinship: How Pair-Bonding Gave Birth to Human Society*. Harvard University Press. https://doi.org/10.4159/97806740 29422.

Charness, G., & Grosskopf, B. (2001). Relative payoffs and happiness: An experimental study. *Journal of Economic Behavior and Organization*, 45, 301–28. https://doi.org/10.1016/S0167-2681(01)00148-2.

Christakis, N. A. (2019). *Blueprint: The Evolutionary Origins of a Good Society*. Little, Brown Spark.

Corning, P. (2011). *The Fair Society: The Science of Human Nature and the Pursuit of Social Justice*. Chicago University Press. https://doi.org/10.7208/ chicago/9780226116303.001.0001.

Corning, P. (2012). *The Fair Society: The Science of Human Nature and the Pursuit of Social Justice*. The University of Chicago Press.

Cosmides, L., & Tooby, J. (2013). Evolutionary psychology: New perspectives on cognition and motivation. *Annual Review of Psychology*, 64, 201–29. https://doi.org/10.1146/annurev.psych.121208.131628.

Courtois, S., Werth, N., Paczkowski, A. et al. (1999). *The Black Book of Communism: Crimes, Terror, Repression*. Harvard University Press.

Csikszentmihalyi, M. (1997a). Evolution and flow. *The NAMTA Journal*, 22(1), 119–49.

Csikszentmihalyi, M. (1997b). Flow and evolution. *The NAMTA Journal*, 22(2), 37–58. https://eric.ed.gov/?id=EJ547967

Csikszentmihalyi, M. (2008). *Flow: The Psychology of Optimal Experience*. Harper Perennial Modern Classics.

Dakin, B. C., Laham, S. M., Tan, N. P.-J., & Bastian, B. (2021). Searching for meaning is associated with costly prosociality. *PLoS ONE*, 16(10), e0258769. https://doi.org/10.1371/journal.pone.0258769.

Darwin, C. (1871). *The Descent of Man, and Selection in Relation to Sex*. John Murray. https://doi.org/110.5962/bhl.title.24784.

Darwin, C. (1874). *The Descent of Man* (2nd ed.). John Murray. https://psy chclassics.yorku.ca/Darwin/Descent/descent4.htm.

Dawkins, R. (1976). *The Selfish Gene*. Oxford University Press.

Dawkins, R., & Wong, Y. (2016). *The Ancestor's Tale: A Pilgrimage to the Dawn of Evolution*. Mariner Books.

De Vos, M. (2012). The unbearable lightness of happiness policy. In P. Booth, ed., *. . . and the Pursuit of Happiness: Wellbeing and the Role of Government*. The Institute of Economic Affairs, pp. 181–200.

de Waal. F. (2010). *The Age of Empathy: Nature's Lessons for a Kinder Society*. Crown Publishers.

Deacon, T. W. (1997). *The Symbolic Species: The Co-evolution of Language and the Brain*. W. W. Norton.

Deaton, A. (2010). Income, aging, health, and well-being around the world: Evidence from the Gallup World Poll. In David A. Wise, ed., *Research Findings in the Economics of Aging*. National Bureau of Economic Research, pp. 235–63. https://doi.org/10.7208/chicago/9780226903088.003.0010

Diener, E. (1984). Subjective well-being. *Psychological Bulletin*, 95(3), 542–75. http://doi.org/10.1037/0033-2909.95.3.542.

Diener, E., ed. (2009a). *Assessing Well-Being: The Collected Works of Ed Diener*. Springer. https://doi.org/10.1007/978-90-481-2354-4.

Diener, E., ed. (2009b). *Culture and Well-Being: The Collected Works of Ed Diener*. Springer. https://doi.org/10.1007/978-90-481-2352-0.

Diener, E. (2009c). Introduction—The science of well-being: Reviews and theoretical articles by Ed Diener. In E. Diener, ed., *The Science of Well-Being: The Collected Works of Ed Diener*. Springer, pp. 1–10. http://doi.org/10.1007/978-90-481-2350-6.

Diener, E., ed. (2009d). *The Science of Well-Being: The Collected Works of Ed Diener*. Springer. https://doi.org/10.1007/978-90-481-2350-6.

Diener, E., Diener, M., & Diener, C. (1995). Factors predicting the subjective well-being of nations. *Journal of Personality and Social Psychology*, 69, 851–64. https://doi.org/10.1037/0022-3514.69.5.851.

Diener, E., Gohm, C., Suh, E., & Oishi, S. (2000). Similarity of the relations between marital status and subjective well-being across cultures. *Journal of Cross-Cultural Psychology*, 31, 419–36. https://doi.org/10.1177/0022022100031004001.

Diener, E., & Lucas, R. E. (1999). Personality and subjective well-being. In D. Kahneman, E. Diener, & N. Schwartz, eds., *Well-Being: The Foundations of Hedonic Psychology*. Russell Sage Foundation, pp. 213–29.

Diener, E., Lucas, R. E., Schimmack, U., & Helliwell, J. F. (2009a). Work, the economy, and well-Being: Policy examples. In E. Diener, R. Lucas, U. Schimmack, & J. Helliwell, eds., *Well-Being for Public Policy*. Oxford University Press, eBook. https://doi.org/10.1093/acprof:oso/9780195334074.001.0001.

Diener, E., Lucas, R. E., & Scollon, C. N. (2009b). Beyond the hedonic treadmill: Revising the adaptation theory of well-being. In E. Diener, ed.,

The Science of Well-Being: The Collected Works of Ed Diener. Springer, pp. 103–18. http://doi.org/10.1007/978-90-481-2350-6_5.

Diener, E., Oishi, S., & Lucas, R. E. (2015). National accounts of subjective well-being. *American Psychologist*, 70(3), 234–42. http://doi.org/10.1037/a0038899.

Diener, E., Sandvik, E., & Pavot, W. (2009c). Happiness is the frequency, not the intensity, of positive versus negative affect. In E. Diener, ed., *Assessing Well-Being: The Collected Works of Ed Diener.* Springer, pp. 213–31. https://doi.org/10.1007/978-90-481-2354-4_10.

Diener, E., & Seligman, M. E. P. (2004). Beyond money: Toward an economy of well-being. *Psychological Science in the Public Interest*, 5(1), 1–31. https://doi.org/10.1111/j.0963-7214.2004.00501001.x.

Dolan, P., Peasgood, T., & White, M. (2008). Do we really know what makes us happy? A review of the economic literature on the factors associated with subjective well-being. *Journal of Economic Psychology*, 29, 94–122. http://doi.org/10.1016/j.joep.2007.09.001.

Dugatkin, L. (1977). *Cooperation among Animals: An Evolutionary Perspective.* Oxford University Press.

Dunbar, R. I. M., & Shultz, S. (2007). Evolution in the social brain. *Science*, 317(5843), 1344–47. https://doi.org/10.1126/science.1145463.

Durand M. (2018). Countries' experiences with well-being and happiness metrics. In *The Global Happiness Council, Global Happiness Policy Report*. Sustainable Development Solutions Network, pp. 200–46. https://s3.amazonaws.com/happinesscouncil.org/GHC_2022.pdf.

Easterlin, R. A. (1974). Does economic growth improve the human lot?: Some empirical evidence. In P. A. David, & M. Abramovitz, eds., *Nations and Households in Economic Growth*. Academic Press, pp. 89–125. http://doi.org/10.1016/B978-0-12-205050-3.50008-7.

Emmons, R., & McCallough, M. (2003). Counting blessings versus burdens: An experimental investigation of gratitude and subjective well-being in daily life. *Journal of Personality and Social Psychology*, 84(2), 377–389.

Foa, R. S., & Mounk, Y. (2019). Youth and the populist wave. *Philosophy and Social Criticism*, 45(9–10), 1013–24. https://doi.org/10.1177/0191453719872314.

Frank, R. H. (1999). *Luxury Fever: Why Money Fails to Satisfy in an Era of Excess*. Free Press.

Frankl, V. E. (1988 [1946]). *Man's Search for Meaning*. Washington Square Press.

Fry, R., & Parker, K. (2021). *Rising Share of U.S. Adults are Living Without a Spouse or Partner*. Pew Research Center. www.pewresearch.org/social-trends/2021/10/05/rising-share-of-u-s-adults-are-living-without-a-spouse-or-partner/.

Gedde-Dahl, M. (2020). En egoistisk middelklasse har sveket resten av samfunnet, mener Paul Collier. *Morgenbladet*. https://www.morgenbladet.no/ideer/2020/11/27/en-egoistisk-middelklasse-har-sveket-resten-av-samfunnet-mener-paul-collier/

Geher, G., & Wedberg, N. (2019). *Positive Evolutionary Psychology: Darwin's Guide to Living a Richer Life*. Oxford University Press. https://doi.org/10.1093/oso/9780190647124.001.0001.

Geher, G., Fritche, M., Goodwine, A., Lombard, J., Longo, K., & Montana, D. (2023). *An Introduction to Positive Evolutionary Psychology*. Oxford University Press. https://doi.org/10.1017/9781009286817.

Gensicke, T. (2000). Freiwilliges Engagement in Den Neuen Ländern. In B. von Rosenbladt, ed., *Ergebnisse Der Repräsentativerhebung 1999 Zu Ehrenamt, Freiwilligenarbeit Und Bürgerschaftliches Engagement [Schriftenreihe Des Bundesministeriums Für Familie, Senioren, Frauen Und Jugend]*. Kohlhammer, pp. 176–85.

Gintis, H. (2008). Punishment and cooperation. *Science*, 319, 1345–6. https://doi.org/10.1126/science.1155333.

Gluckman, P., & Hanson, M. (2006). *Mismatch: Why Our World No Longer Fits Our Bodies*. Oxford University Press.

Goldin, I. (2018). The problems with Steven Pinker's optimism. *Nature*, 554, 420–22. www.nature.com/articles/d41586-018-02148-1.

Gruber, J., Mauss, I. B., & Tamir, M. (2011). A dark side of happiness? How, when, and why happiness is not always good. *Perspectives on Psychological Science*, 6, 222. https://doi.org/10.1177/1745691611406927.

Guglielmo, S., Monroe, A. E., & Malle, B. F. (2009). At the heart of morality lies folk psychology. *Inquiry*, 52, 449–66. https://doi.org/10.1080/00201740903302600.

Haidt, J. (2006). *The Happiness Hypothesis: Finding Modern Truth in Ancient Wisdom*. Basic Books.

Harari, Y. N. (2014). *Sapiens: A Brief History of Humankind*. Random House.

Harari, Y. N. (2016). *Homo Deus: A Brief History of Tomorrow*. Harvill Secker. https://doi.org/10.17104/9783406704024.

Hayes, S. C., Hofmann, S. G., & Wilson, D. S. (2020). Clinical psychology is an applied evolutionary science. *Clinical Psychology Review*, 81, 101892. https://doi.org/10.1016/j.cpr.2020.101892.

Hellevik, O. (2008). *Jakten på den norske lykken: Norsk monitor 1985–2007*. Universitetsforlaget.

Hellevik, O. (2011). Inntekt og subjektiv livskvalitet: Easterlins paradoks. *Tidsskrift for velferdsforskning*, 14(3), 181–203.

Hellevik, O., & Hellevik, T. (2021). Hvorfor ser færre unge lyst på livet? *Nordisk tidsskrift for ungdomsforskning*, 2(2), 104–28. https://doi.org/10.18261/issn.2535-8162-2021-02-02.

Helliwell, J. F., Layard, R., Sachs, J. D., De Neve, J. -E., Aknin, L. B., & Wang, S. (2022). *World Happiness Report 2022*. Sustainable Development Solutions Network. https://worldhappiness.report/ed/2022/.

Helliwell, J., & Huang, H. F. (2008). How's your government? International evidence linking good government and well-being. *British Journal of Political Science*, 38, 595–619. https://doi.org/10.1017/S0007123408000306.

Henrich, H. (2017). *The Secret of Our Success: How Evolution Is Driving Human Development, Domesticating Our Species and Making Us Smarter*. Princeton University Press.

Henrich, J. (2020). *The WEIRDest People in the World: How the West Became Psychologically Peculiar and Particularly Prosperous*. Farrar, Straus and Giroux.

Henrich, J., Heine, S. J., & Norenzayan, A. (2010). The Weirdest people in the world? *Behavioral and Brain Sciences*, 33(2–3), 61–83. https://doi.org/10.1017/S0140525X0999152X.

Hickel, J. (2020). *Less Is More: How Degrowth Will Save the World*. Random House.

Hill, R. A., & Dunbar, R. I. M. (2003). Social network size in humans. *Human Nature*, 14(1), 53–72. https://doi.org/10.1007/s12110-003-1016-y.

Hill, S. E., & Buss, D. M. (2006). Envy and positional bias in the evolutionary psychology of management. *Managerial and Decision Economics*, 27, 131–43. https://doi.org/10.1002/mde.1288.

Hill, S. E., & Buss, D. M. (2008). Evolution and subjective well-being. In M. Eid, & R. J. Larsen, eds., *The Science of Subjective Well-Being*. The Guilford Press, pp. 62–79.

Hillman, J. (1994). Psychology, self and community. *Resurgence*, 20, 18–21.

Hitokoto, H., & Uchida, Y. (2015). Interdependent happiness: Theoretical importance and measurement validity. *Journal of Happiness Studies*, 16, 211–39. https://doi.org/10.1007/s10902-014-9505-8.

Hofstede Insights (2019). Country Comparison. www.hofstede-insights.com.

Holmes, M., & McKenzie, J. (2019). Relational happiness through recognition and redistribution: Emotion and inequality. *European Journal of Social Theory*, 22(4), 439–574. https://doi.org/10.1177/1368431018799257.

Hui, B. P. H., Ng, J. C. K., Berzaghi, E., Cunningham-Amos, L. A., & Kogan, A. (2020). Rewards of kindness? A meta-analysis of the link between prosociality and well-being. *Psychological Bulletin*, 146(12), 1084–116. http://doi.org/10.1037/bul0000298.

Huizinga, J. (2016). *Homo Ludens: A Study of the Play-Element in Culture.* Martino Fine Books.

Huppert, F. A. (2014). The state of wellbeing science: Concepts, measures, interventions, and policies. In F. A. Huppert, & C. L. Cooper, eds., *Interventions and Policies to Enhance Wellbeing: Wellbeing: A Complete Reference Guide, Volume VI.* Wiley, eBook. https://doi.org/10.1002/9781118539415.wbwell036.

Huppert, F. A., Marks, N., Clark, A., et al. (2009). Measuring well-being across Europe: Description of the ESS well-being module and preliminary findings. *Social Indicators Research*, 91(3), 301–15. https://doi.org/10.1007/s11205-008-9346-0.

Joshanloo, M., & Weijers, D. (2014). Aversion to happiness across cultures: A review of where and why people are averse to happiness. *Journal of Happiness Studies*, 15, 717–35. http://doi.org/10.1007/s10902-013-9489-9.

Kahneman, D., Diener, E., & Schwarz. N. , eds. (1999). *Wellbeing: The Foundations of Hedonic Psychology.* Russell Sage Foundation.

Keltner, D. (2009). *Born to Be Good: The Science of a Meaningful Life.* Norton.

Keyes, C. L. M., Kendler, K. S., Myers, J. M., & Martin, C. C. (2015). The genetic overlap and distinctiveness of flourishing and the big five personality traits. *Journal of Happiness Studies*, 16(3), 655–68. http://doi.org/10.1007/s10902-014-9527-2.

Khademi, R., & Najafi, M. (2020). Tracing the historical roots of positive psychology by reference publication year spectroscopy (RPYS): A scientometrics perspective. *Current Psychology*, 39, 438–44. https://doi.org/10.1007/s12144-018-0044-z.

Kirkpatrick, L. A., & Navarrete, C. D. (2010). Reports of my death anxiety have been greatly exaggerated: A critique of terror management theory from an evolutionary perspective. *Psychological Inquiry*, 17(4), 288–98. https://doi.org/10.1080/10478400701366969.

Klostermaier, K. K. (2004). Moksa. In S. Mittal & Gene Thursby, eds., *The Hindu World*. Routledge, pp. 288–305.

Konow, J., & Earley, J. (2002). *The Hedonistic Paradox: Is Homo Economicus Happier?* Mimeo, Loyola Marymount University.

Kornai, J. (2021). *The Socialist System: The Political Economy of Communism.* Princeton University Press. https://doi.org/10.2307/j.ctv1ddczdr.

Kornai, J., Rothstein, B., & Rose-Ackerman, S., eds. (2004). *Creating Social Trust in Post-Socialist Transition*. Palgrave Macmillan. https://doi.org/10.1057/9781403980663.

Krastev, I., & Holmes, S. (2020). *The Light that Failed: A Reckoning*. Penguin Books.

Krys, K., Capaldi, C. A., Zelenski, J. M., et al. (2021a). Family well-being is valued more than personal well-being: A four-country study. *Current Psychology*, 40, 3332–43. http://doi.org/10.1007/s12144-019-00249-2

Krys, K., Park, J., Kocimska-Zych, A. et al. (2021b). Personal life satisfaction as a measure of societal happiness is an individualistic presumption: Evidence from fifty countries. *Journal of Happiness Studies*, 22, 2197–214. http://doi.org/10.1007/s10902-020-00311-y.

Kuppuswamy, B. (1977). *Dharma and Society*. The Macmillan Company of India.

Kuti, E. (2004). Civic service in Eastern Europe and Central Asia: From mandatory public work toward civic service. *Nonprofit and Voluntary Sector Quarterly*, 33(4), 79S–97S. https://doi.org/10.1177/0899764004269740.

Larsen, M. (2020). Agreeing on history: Adaptation as restorative truth in Finnish reconciliation. *Literature/Film Quarterly*, 48(1).

Larsen, M. (2021). The Lutheran imaginary that underpins social democracy. *Frontiers in Psychology*, 12, 746406. https://doi.org/10.3389/fpsyg.2021.746406.

Larsen, M. (2022). *Bridging the Narrative Abyss: Evolution toward Social Democracy in a Millennium of Nordic Fiction*. Dissertation, University of California, Los Angeles.

Larsen, M. (2023). Americanizing the Scandinavian super underdog in eighteen film remakes. *Journal of Film and Video*, 75(1), 29–45. https://doi.org/10.5406/19346018.75.1.03.

Larsen, M., & Witoszek, N. (2023). Strategies of prosociality: Comparing Nordic and Slavonic altruism toward Ukrainian refugees. *Frontiers in Psychology*, 14, 1065889. https://doi.org/10.3389/fpsyg.2023.1065889.

Larsen, M., Witoszek, N., & Yeung, J. C. (2023). A multilevel selection model for prosocial well-being. *Frontiers in Psychology*, 14, 1068119. https://doi.org/10.3389/fpsyg.2023.1068119.

Levi, P. (1996). *Survival in Auschwitz*. Touchstone.

Lewis, D. M. G., Al-Shawaf, L., Russell, E. M., & Buss, D. M. (2015). Friends and happiness: An evolutionary perspective on friendship. In M. Demir, ed., *Friendship and Happiness*. Springer, pp. 37–57. http://doi.org/10.1007/978-94-017-9603-3_3.

Lyubomirsky, S., Sheldon, K. M., & Schkade, D. (2005). Pursuing happiness: The architecture of sustainable change. *Review of General Psychology*, 9, 111–31. https://doi.org/10.1037/1089-2680.9.2.111.

McKie, R. (2010). My bright idea: humans found a nicer way to evolve. *The Guardian*. www.theguardian.com/technology/2010/sep/19/evolution-frans-de-waal-primatologist.

McMahon, D. M. (2006). *Happiness: A History.* Grove Press.

Meier, S., & Stutzer, A. (2008). Is volunteering rewarding in itself? *Economica*, 75(297), 39–59. https://doi.org/10.1111/j.1468-0335.2007.00597.x.

Mendis, P. (1994). Buddhist economics and community development strategies. *Community Development Journal*, 29(3), 195–202. https://doi.org/10.1093/cdj/29.3.195.

Midgley, M. (2010). *The Solitary Self: Darwin and the Selfish Gene.* Routledge. https://doi.org/10.1017/UPO9781844654833.

Milanović, B. (2017). The illusion of "degrowth" in a poor and unequal world. *Globalinequality.* http://glineq.blogspot.com/2017/11/the-illusion-of-degrowth-in-poor-and.html

Moche, H., & Västfjäll, D. (2021). To give or to take money? The effects of choice on prosocial spending and happiness. *Journal of Positive Psychology*, 17(5), 742–53. https://doi.org/10.1080/17439760.2021.1940248.

Musick, M. A., & Wilson, J. (2003). Volunteering and depression: The role of psychological and social resources in different age groups. *Social Science and Medicine*, 56, 259–69. http://doi.org/10.1016/S0277-9536(02)00025-4.

Myerson, A. (1917). Eupathics: A program for mental hygiene. *The Journal of Abnormal Psychology*, 12(5), 343–7. http://doi:10.1037/h0073646.

Nesse, R. M. (2005). Natural selection and the elusiveness of happiness. In F. A. Huppert, N. Baylis, & B. Keverne, eds., *The Science of Well-Being.* Oxford University Press, eBook. http://doi.org/10.1093/acprof:oso/9780198567523.003.0001.

O'Day, E. B., & Heimberg, R. G. (2021). Social media use, social anxiety, and loneliness: A systematic review. *Computers in Human Behavior Reports*, 3, 100070. https://doi.org/10.1016/j.chbr.2021.100070.

Oakley, B., Knafo, A., Madhavan, G., & Wilson, D. S., eds. (2011). *Pathological Altruism.* Oxford University Press. https://doi.org/10.1093/acprof:oso/9780199738571.001.0001.

Oishi, S., & Diener, E. (2014). Residents of poor nations have a greater sense of meaning in life than residents of wealthy nations. *Psychological Science*, 25(2), 422–30. http://doi.org/10.1177/0956797613507286.

Oishi, S., Diener, E., & Lucas, R. E. (2009). The optimum level of well-being: Can people be too happy? In E. Diener, ed., *The Science of Well-Being: The Collected Works of Ed Diener.* Springer, pp. 175–200. https://doi.org/10.1007/978-90-481-2350-6_8.

Our World in Data (2019). Percentage of one-person households, 1960 to 2018. https://ourworldindata.org/grapher/one-person-households.

Oxford Reference. (2024). Prosocial behaviour. www.oxfordreference.com/view/10.1093/oi/authority.20110803100350224.

Parel, A. J. (2008). Gandhi and the emergence of the modern Indian political canon. *The Review of Politics*, 70(1), 40–63. https://doi.org/10.1017/S0034670508000041.

Pawełczyńska, A. (1979). *Values and Violence in Auschwitz: A Sociological Analysis*. University of California Press.

Piliavin, J. A. (2003). Doing well by doing good: Benefits for the benefactor. In C. L. M. Keyes & J. Haidt, eds., *Flourishing: Positive Psychology and the Life Well-Lived*. American Psychological Association, pp. 227–47. http://doi.org/10.1037/10594-010.

Pinker, S. (2012). *The Better Angels of Our Nature: Why Violence Has Declined*. Penguin.

Pinker, S. (2015). The false allure of group selection. In D. M. Buss, ed., *The Handbook of Evolutionary Psychology*, vol. 2. Wiley, pp. 867–80. https://doi.org/10.1002/9781119125563.evpsych236.

Pinker, S. (2019). *Enlightenment Now: The Case for Reason, Science, Humanism, and Progress*. Penguin.

Plagnol, A. C., & Huppert, F. A. (2010). Happy to help? Exploring the factors associated with variations in rates of volunteering across Europe. *Social Indicators Research*, 97, 157–76. https://doi.org/10.1007/s11205-009-9494-x.

Pollen, M. (2018) *How To Change Your Mind: What the New Science of Psychedelics Teaches Us About Consciousness, Dying, Addiction, Depression, and Transcendence*. Penguin.

Popper, K. R. (2020 [1945]). *The Open Society and Its Enemies*. Princeton University Press. https://doi.org/10.1515/9780691212067.

Rappleye, J., Komatsu, H., Uchida, Y., Krys, K., & Markus, H. (2020). "Better policies for better lives"?: Constructive critique of the OECD's (mis)measure of student well-being. *Journal of Education Policy*, 35(2), 258–82. http://doi.org/10.1080/02680939.2019.1576923.

Reed, P., & Rothenberg, D. (1993). *Wisdom of the Open Air: The Norwegian Roots of Deep Ecology*. University of Minnesota Press.

Renton, A. (2015). What would you pay to be happy? *The Guardian*. www.theguardian.com/society/2015/may/10/what-would-you-pay-to-be-happy.

Ricard, M. (2015). *Altruism*. Little, Brown.

Richerson, P., & Boyd, R. (2005). Not by Genes Alone: How Culture Transformed Human Evolution, University of Chicago Press.

Røysamb, E., & Nes, R. B. (2016). Genes, environments, and core features of eudaimonic wellbeing. In J. Vittersø, ed., *Handbook of Eudaimonic Well-Being*. Springer, pp. 233–52. http://doi.org/10.1007/978-3-319-42445-3_16.

Røysamb, E., & Nes, R. B. (2018). The genetics of wellbeing. In E. Diener, S. Oishi, & L. Tay, eds., *Handbook of Well-Being*. DEF Publishers, eBook.

Różycka-Tran, J., Piotrowski, J. P., Żemojtel-Piotrowska, M., et al. (2021). Belief in a zero-sum game and subjective well-being across 35 countries. *Current Psychology*, 40, 3575–84. https://doi.org/10.1007/s12144-019-00291-0.

Ryan, R. M., & Deci, E. L. (2017). *Self-Determination Theory: Basic Psychological Needs in Motivation, Development, and Wellness*. The Guildford Press. https://doi.org/10.1521/978.14625/28806.

Seligman, M. E. P. (2002). *Authentic Happiness: Using the New Positive Psychology to Realize Your Potential for Lasting Fulfillment*. Free Press.

Seligman, M. E. P. (2000). Positive psychology. In M. Seligman, & J. Gillham, eds., *The Science of Optimism and Hope: Research Essays in Honor of Martin E.P. Seligman*. Templeton Foundation Press, pp. 415–29.

Sen, A. K. (1993). Capability and well-being. In M. C. Nussbaum, & A. K. Sen, eds., *The Quality of Life*. Oxford University Press, pp. 30–53. https://doi.org/10.1093/0198287976.003.0003.

Sen, A. K. (2016). Amartya Sen on Cultural Relativism and 'the good life'. Berggruen Institute, YouTube, www.youtube.com/watch?v=ZwAxj5mnVRI.

Sennett, R. (2013). *Together: The Rituals, Pleasures, and Politics of Cooperation*. Yale University Press.

Silk, J. B., Brosnan, S. F., Vonk, J., et al. (2005). Chimpanzees are indifferent to the welfare of unrelated group members. *Nature*, 437(7063), 1357–9. https://doi.org/10.1038/nature04243.

Smith, N. (2021). People are realizing that degrowth is bad. *Noahpinion*. https://www.noahpinion.blog/p/people-are-realizing-that-degrowth

Sober, E., & Wilson, D. S. (2013). *Unto Others: The Evolution Theory of Unselfish Behavior*. Harvard University Press.

Solomon, S., Greenberg, J., & Pyszczynski, T. (2000). Pride and prejudice: Fear of death and social behavior. *Current Directions in Psychological Science*, 9(6), 200–4. https://doi.org/10.1111/1467-8721.00094.

SSB (2021). *Nok en gang rekordlav fruktbarhet*. Statistics Norway. www.ssb.no/befolkning/artikler-og-publikasjoner/nok-en-gang-rekordlav-fruktbarhet.

Stevenson, B., & Wolfers, J. (2008). Economic growth and subjective well-being: Reassessing the Easterlin paradox. *Brookings Papers on Economic Activity*, 39(1), 1–102. http://doi.org/10.1353/eca.0.0001.

Strack, F., Schwarz, N., Kern, C., and Wagner, D. (1990). The salience of comparison standards and the activation of social norms: Consequences for judgments of happiness and their communication. *Br. J. Soc. Psychol.* 29, 303–314. doi: 10.1111/j.2044-8309.1990.tb00912.x

Suarez, S. D., & Gallup, G. G. (1985). Depression as a response to reproductive failure. *Journal of Social and Biological Structures*, 8(3), 279–87. https://doi.org/10.1016/0140-1750(85)90071-5.

Thoits, P. A., & Hewitt, L. N. (2001). Volunteer work and well-being. *Journal of Health and Social Behavior*, 42(2), 115–31. http://doi.org/10.2307/3090173.

Turchin, P. (2007). *War and Peace and War: The Rise and Fall of Empires*. Plume.

Turkle, S. (2012). *Alone Together: Why We Expect More from Technology and Less from Each Other*. Basic Books.

Uchida, Y., & Kitayama, S. (2009). Happiness and unhappiness in east and west: Themes and variations. *Emotion*, 9(4), 441–56. http://doi.org/10.1037/a0015634.

Uchida, Y., Norasakkunkit, V. & Kitayama, S. (2004). Cultural constructions of happiness: theory and empirical evidence. *Journal of Happiness Studies*, 5, 223–39. https://doi.org/10.1007/s10902-004-8785-9.

Uchida, Y., Townsend, S. S. M., Markus, H. R., & Bergsieker, H. B. (2009). Emotions as within or between people? Cultural variation in lay theories of emotion expression and inference. *PSPB*, 35(11), 1427–39. http://doi.org/10.1177/0146167209347322.

Vaillant, G. E. (2009). *Spiritual Evolution: How We Are Wired for Faith, Hope, and Love*. Broadway Books.

Warneken, F., & Tomasello, M. (2009). The roots of human altruism. *British Journal of Psychology*, 100, 455–71. https://doi.org/10.1348/000712608X379061.

Weiss, A., Bates, T. C., & Luciano, M. (2008). Happiness is a personal(ity) thing: The genetics of personality and well-being in a representative sample. *Psychological Science*, 19(3), 205–10. http://doi.org/10.1111/j.1467-9280.2008.02068.x.

Welzel, C. (2013). *Freedom Rising: Human Empowerment and the Quest for Emancipation*. Cambridge University Press. https://doi.org/10.1017/CBO9781139540919.

White, S. C. (2017). Relational wellbeing: Re-centring the politics of happiness, policy and the self. *Policy & Politics*, 45(2), 121–36. https://doi.org/10.1332/030557317X14866576265970.

Wilson, D. S. (2015) *Does Altruism Exist? Culture, Genes, and the Welfare of Others*. Yale University Press.

Wilson, D. S. (2007). *Evolution for Everyone: How Darwin's Theory Can Change the Way We Think about Our Lives*. Delacorte Press.

Wilson, D. S. (2016). *Does Altruism Exist Culture, Genes and the Welfare of Others*. Yale University Press.

Wilson, D. S. (2019). *This View of Life: Completing the Darwinian Revolution.* Pantheon Books.

Wilson, D. S., Hayes, S. C., Biglan, A., & Embry, D. D. (2014). Evolving the future: Toward a science of intentional change. *Behavioral and Brain Sciences*, 37(4), 395–416. http://doi:10.1017/S0140525X13001593.

Wilson, D. S., & Hessen, D. O. (2018). Cooperation, competition, and multi-level selection: A new paradigm for understanding the Nordic Model. In N. Witoszek & A. Midttun, eds., *Sustainable Modernity: The Nordic Model and Beyond*. Routledge, pp. 18–35. http://doi.org/10.4324/9781315195964-2.

Wilson, D. S., & Wilson, E. O. (2007). Evolution: Survival of the selfless. *New Scientist*, 196(2628), 42–6. https://doi.org/10.1016/S0262-4079(07)62792-4.

Wilson, W. (1967). Correlates of avowed happiness. *Psychological Bulletin*, 67(4), 294–306. http://doi:10.1037/h0024431.

Winkelmann, L., & Winkelmann, R. (2010). Does inequality harm the middle-class? *Kyklos*, 63(2), 301–16. https://doi.org/10.1111/j.1467-6435.2010.00474.x.

Witoszek, N. (2011). *The Origins of the Regime of Goodness. Remapping the Norwegian Cultural History.* Scandinavian University Press.

Witoszek, N. (2012). *The Origins of the Regime of Goodness: Remapping Norwegian Cultural History.* Universitetsforlaget.

Witoszek, N., & Midttun, A., eds. (2018). *Sustainable Modernity: The Nordic Model and Beyond*. Routledge. https://doi.org/10.4324/9781315195964.

Witoszek, N., & Sørensen, Ø. (2018). Nordic humanism as a driver of the welfare society. In N. Witoszek & A. Midttun, eds., *Sustainable Modernity: The Nordic Model and Beyond*. Routledge, pp. 36–58. https://doi.org/10.4324/9781315195964-3.

Woodcock, G., & Avakumović, I. (1950). *The Anarchist Prince: A Biography of Prince Peter Kropotkin*. Boardman Books.

Wooldridge, A. (2020). Visors and violence: We are returning to the middle ages. *The Economist*. www.economist.com/1843/2020/09/14/visors-and-violence-we-are-returning-to-the-middle-ages.

Wrangham, R. W. (2019a). Hypotheses for the evolution of reduced reactive aggression in the context of human self-domestication. *Frontiers in Psychology*, 10, 1914. https://doi.org/10.3389/fpsyg.2019.01914.

Wrangham, R. (2019b). *The Goodness Paradox: The Strange Relationship between Virtue and Violence in Human Evolution*. Pantheon.

Zuboff, S. (2018). *The Age of Surveillance Capitalism*. Harvard University Press.

Funding Statement

This Element was written as part of the multinational "Grieg" project, which is supported by a European Economic Area grant (project number 2019/34/H/HS6/00597).

Cambridge Elements ☰

Applied Evolutionary Science

David F. Bjorklund
Florida Atlantic University

David F. Bjorklund is a Professor of Psychology at Florida Atlantic University in Boca Raton, Florida. He is the Editor-in-Chief of the *Journal of Experimental Child Psychology*, the Vice President of the Evolution Institute, and has written numerous articles and books on evolutionary developmental psychology, with a particular interest in the role of immaturity in evolution and development.

Editorial Board

About the Series

This series presents original, concise, and authoritative reviews of key topics in applied evolutionary science. Highlighting how an evolutionary approach can be applied to real-world social issues, many Elements in this series will include findings from programs that have produced positive educational, social, economic, or behavioral benefits. Cambridge Elements in Applied Evolutionary Science is published in association with the Evolution Institute.

 THE EVOLUTION INSTITUTE

Cambridge Elements ⁼

Applied Evolutionary Science

Printed in the United States
by Baker & Taylor Publisher Services